Praise for **A Unique Renega**

"In *A Unique Renegade*, Mike is guiding you to your ultimate greatness, inviting you on a trip to personal growth and intellectual awakening. This book is a powerful reminder of what we all are capable of when we dare to manifest our deepest dreams. Read it and learn how to create the life you always wanted."

    – Anca Maria Dumitrescu, author of *Journey – An Outlined Path to Fulfillment*

"*A Unique Renegade* encourages us to take a deeper look at ourselves and our lives. It provides personal stories and examples to help us examine our issues and understand that within every problem, there lies a solution and inspires us to find the courage we need, to make the changes we must, in order to live the lives we want to live."

    – Colleen Aynn, #1 International Best-Selling Author of *Sad Sally* and the *Feeling Friends*

"*A Unique Renegade* is a book which teaches you how to be the Unique Renegade that you are. Mike Tate discusses why most of us are stuck in our lives and goes into detail to explain why conformity with society's expectations hampers rather than helps us. Competition is a killer: in order to be a Unique Renegade, we need to create rather than compete. Uniqueness comes from understanding who you are, what's controlling you and being aware so that you can move forward in your life. If you'd like to learn more about being the creator that you are, do yourself a favor: read the book and take action!"

    – Joanne Ong

"Learn, get clear, and delve deep into self-growth terms and tools. Create your excellent life by applying Mike Tate's knowledge and wisdom, and start your change of a lifetime."

    –Inbal Hillel

EFFECTIVELY AND EFFORTLESSLY
MASTER YOUR LIFE

A UNIQUE
RENEGADE

Caleb,
Best to you on your journey!
Mike T

MIKE TATE

auniquerenegade.com

Published by Hasmark Publishing, judy@hasmarkservices.com

Copyright © 2017 Michael Tate First Edition, 2017

Editor, Sigrid Macdonald
http://www.bookmagic.ca/

Cover Design, Killer Covers
http://killercovers.com

Book Design, Anne Karklins
annekarklins@gmail.com

ISBN 978-1-988071-82-4
ISBN 1988071828

ACKNOWLEDGMENTS

This has been an amazing journey. I have learned from some of the best in the industry. I'd like to take this opportunity to offer my appreciation to the people I have gained so much understanding from. This has expanded me as a person.

First and foremost, I'd like to thank my mentor during the book writing process, Peggy McColl. Her absolute support and faith in me have driven me from a 10-year-old idea to this finished product. She is THE subject matter expert in the book writing and launching industry. I have worked with her personally and can affirm that she is as authentic as they come. She is often heard saying that everyone has a book inside them. If you do, contact Peggy to make your dream a reality. She is very qualified as a *New York Times* Best Seller and author of many programs to help you get your book out to the world.

Bob Proctor is another mentor from whom I have gained much understanding about the Laws of the Universe. He is the foremost authority on Personal Development and Co-founder of the Proctor Gallagher Institute. I have been to Bob's events and spoken with him personally on my journey to learning how we can improve ourselves if we will just focus on what is important to us. His influence on this industry dates back over 50 years, and he has stated he will do this until the last minute.

I would also like to mention my Toastmasters mentors, Rick Taylor and Sawyer Smith. Between these two, I have learned much about public speaking on my journey to the Toastmasters Competent Communicator designation. Being able to communicate effectively is no longer optional;

it is a required skill in Personal Development and many other industries. Regarding this same subject, I met Colleen Aynn at one of Peggy McColl's mentorship seminars in Canada, and she introduced us to her "Epic System" of delivering a presentation with maximum impact. I was wise enough to volunteer when she asked us who would, and I learned more simple and powerful ways of commanding attention while speaking in public.

Finally, I appreciate YOU, one of the many millions of people whom I hope will be inspired by this book. It was written for you. My deepest desire is that even *one idea* in this book takes you one step closer to the life of your dreams!

DEDICATION

In dedicating this book, I want to express appreciation for the privilege of being a dad and mentor for two of the finest young men I know. This journey was far from the typical story of being a "parent." My sons had chosen to live with me, making me a rare breed of parent known as the single dad. I learned so much from Mikey Tate and Kenny Tate from this experience that we could (and will... hint, hint) write an entire book about how this unique partnership blossomed into the lifetime relationship that it did.

Mikey was the first to move in with me, and it was clear from very early on that we would learn so much from each other. He is mostly self-taught and has always made his own way even when it was not easy. He currently works in the IT field and enjoys gaming, travel, and computer technology. His first internship was at 15 years old, tracking and installing servers with me in the data center I worked in at that time. They learn so easily when it is not a requirement but an offer to see something new.

Kenny was the second to move in and experienced a miracle shortly after doing so. He had been "diagnosed" with lazy eye. This had him in glasses, which is something I did not think should be necessary. We had talked about how well HE thought he was seeing. He stopped wearing the glasses a week or two after he moved in and has not needed them since! Then, as soon as we moved to Arlington, Virginia, he landed a job selling Blu-Ray players at Best Buy at 17 years old. He saved up and bought himself a NICE gaming laptop.

What amazes me about these two is how they don't let other opinions or diagnoses stand in their way. The public educational system had said they are autistic, and that turned out to be a compliment. The truth is they are very gifted and think differently than their peers. They are both ahead of their peers as this is written and the future for them shows no limits. It has been a true inspiration to learn from these two. If you want it, can see it, and believe it, it will be yours. They are living proof. I love you, my sons.

TABLE OF CONTENTS

FOREWORD

A Unique Renegade is one of the first self-help books that focuses on Personal Development and how to use it to improve your overall life. The book starts with principles that are essential to your happiness and success and then builds upon them. Once you understand these principles, you will understand what you really want as you do have the power to go after it. This book will enlighten you to discover your own path.

In an era where there are hundreds of thousands of "self-help" books, many of them based on popular culture and trends, this book contains gifts that are timeless. The concepts are clearly presented in a respectful voice, by an author obviously intelligent, inquiring, creative, daring and well-educated.

Mike teaches the reader about the Laws of Vibration, Polarity, and Attraction and how to apply them to your life. He communicates that when a person starts accepting responsibility for the choices he makes in his life, he unleashes a power from within. He explains that by empowering yourself, you will actually be inspiring others.

> *"Plant the seed of what you want in your mind*
> *to get what you want out of life."*
> – Mike Tate

There are many excuses that we tell ourselves that prevent us from being truly happy, and within these pages, you will learn how to move past them. This book has the ability to free you from your own self-imposed self-concepts. It is filled with powerful truths. But the truths are not there to beat you over the head with complex sounding terms. They are explained with simple words, and this ease of expression makes the book powerful and ready for a huge audience.

Not only is the content incredible and highly actionable, but it may also force you to dig deeper and make the positive change you desire. Mike lays out the most direct personal guidance and insight for an individual to find and work to reach her or his full potential.

> *The most valuable gift you can give to yourself*
> *and those around you is to be your authentic self.*
> – Mike Tate

What I really like about this book is that it's not just a "feel good" read. It's something that can be personal to each reader and really make a long-lasting impact. Knowledge is the quickest and safest path to success in any area of life.

The author stresses that it is thinking that rules emotions, not the other way around. When I was able to recognize my own negative thinking, I was then able to reverse it before it immobilized me.

A Unique Renegade reinforces the power that is within each and everyone. It will encourage anyone to think positive, never give up, and keep working hard toward your purpose to fulfill your destiny.

Like a patient teacher, it takes your hand and walks you through precisely what it means to live a life based on joy. And what a delightful, refreshing, thought-provoking and, ultimately, life-changing stroll it is.

Remember, knowledge alone isn't power; applied knowledge is power. Mike has provided you with a wealth of knowledge, stories, and experiences for you to draw from. Now it's time for you to apply it to your life.

Read it for the light it can bring. Live it for the positive changes it can invoke. Love it for the joy you can share and experience.

Peggy McColl, *New York Times* Best-Selling Author
http://PeggyMcColl.com

WELCOME

Welcome to *A Unique Renegade*. You are most likely reading this book because you want to have a life experience more to your liking. You have probably let what you are "supposed" to do be more important than what you want to do. There are so many things that attract our attention in life, it becomes a constant process to try and determine what is or is not right for you. You have probably heard "the struggle is real" one too many times, maybe even from yourself! It does not have to be that way. If you want to get to the point of an expanding, good feeling life, you are reading the right material.

As we look around, everyone seems to be harping on responsibility. In truth, there is only one responsibility, and it is to yourself. With proper thought processes, self-responsibility leads to responsibility in all other areas of life. You determine how any subject makes you feel, so it only makes sense that you are the one who creates your overall attitude toward life. This is true because you are the only one who can think for yourself. You can allow other opinions or your own to dictate your behavior. It is all under your control.

I have had many situations, some detailed in this book, where I have applied the processes presented here to produce an increase or quantum leap for my or the life of someone close to me. As you will discover, there are science and Divine Law behind these processes, and you can leverage them to create the life you truly want to live. Everyone on earth has desires that they believe will help them feel better. A relatively small percentage see these desires move into reality. You can and deserve to be one of those people fulfilling your dreams and inspiring others while doing so.

This book has been written to get you started on shifting your attention toward circumstances, events, people and things that will help you find your own journey to empowerment. Empowered people evolve from empowered minds. They embrace their desires. They focus on what they want and find access to it easily. They inspire others, thereby inspiring themselves. The people around them follow their path to success through inspiration. They are the inventors. They are the creators. They are the people who have it just the way they want it. By empowering yourself through your own mind, you start to bring the true essence of who you REALLY are to the surface. You were born with the ability to live a beautifully full, abundant life. By following the desire in your heart, you can be where you WANT to be. You deserve to be there, too. You CAN effortlessly and effectively be the Master of Your Own Life.

BECOME A UNIQUE RENEGADE

Renegade (noun): a person who deserts a party or cause for another.

Desert what everyone else wants for you for what YOU want for you. When you can say to yourself, "I am A Unique Renegade. Nobody tells me how to think." and mean it, you can change your life. Since you are reading this, and have gotten this far, it is time to take your life back. YOU are THE MOST important person in your own life. Become A Unique Renegade. Empower yourself! It is time to uniquely and effectively master your own life. I would encourage you to just consider this: What inspires you?

Does more wealth inspire you?

Does creating your OWN prosperity inspire you?

Does more happiness inspire you?

Does better health inspire you?

Do better relationships inspire you?

You have very likely been looking and seeking outside yourself for all of this. Most people allow external influence to control a lot of their lives. News, politics, stress and the resulting worry all create negative thoughts and emotions inside these people. They are simply offering much of their attention to what they don't want. That attention plays a significant role in bringing the unwanted to these people.

As a specific example, the news is designed more to enrich the sponsors than empower its audience with information that will inspire them to greater things. The stories being created are almost always about what's wrong with the world. There seems to be a war or opposition to values or anything political. So many of these elitist people think that their beliefs are right for everyone and know how all people should live, so they attempt to bombard everyone they can with how they should think and live. Preaching fear religiously and in the news is a HUGE part of this. Believing all of these stories based on fear can lead to a person experiencing stress. As the stress takes hold, doubt and worry come into play. Then these people can literally worry themselves sick. This becomes true because as they worry, their bodies feel less at ease. This can progress to being vulnerable to dis-ease. Conversely, an emotionally healthy body is VERY resistant to dis-ease. This is why the news is so irrelevant to me. I make my OWN news. I don't get sick that often, and if I do get a diagnosis I don't want, I focus on HEAL-THY versus dis-ease. I recommend others do, too. Life is better and more free this way. You can find good news via the internet, by getting books like this one, or by making your own and writing about it for all to see. The vast majority of people have no idea about the infinite power inside them that can make their lives all that they want them to be through a simple shift in their awareness. Ask yourself the following questions:

Does what you are usually focused on truly inspire you?

How much influence do you have on most of your own thought? Where does it come from?

Now, consider this: What is it that influences most of your thought?

Do you use other news, groups, and other people's opinions to validate your own beliefs?

If the source of the answers to any of these questions leads you anywhere but inside yourself, it is time to shift your perspective. It is time to become A Unique Renegade in today's world. Society's Renegades think about what they will get and get what they think about. Every time. Without exception. They are the people who are creating most of the positive change in the world. They empower others by being empowered themselves. Their success is the result of the combination of an absolute understanding of Divine Law, desire driven by clear vision and achieving their goals.

Influential Renegades

There are many amazing examples of people who are very inspiring. They deserted what others wanted for them for what they wanted for themselves and the world. These people aligned with *the voice inside them* instead of giving any attention to all of the outside voices to guide them. As Dr. John

Demartini famously said, "When the voice and the vision on the inside become more profound and more clear and loud than the opinions on the outside, you've mastered your life." There are so many people who mastered theirs and changed countless others. Let's look at some groups of the population that are well-known for producing Influential Renegades.

The Information Technology World

Research will show many founders of the most successful technology companies on earth are people who deserted what others wanted for them for what they envisioned for the world. From the technology we use to the way we interface with each other, these Unique Renegades have led the way in changing how the world communicates. What used to be an expensive, overseas phone call can now be carried over many FREE messaging services. People can communicate across oceans and continents as easily as making a local phone call. The founders of many of these organizations chose their own visions over the vision that their colleges had for them and forged a path that changed the world forever.

Other Industries

Dating back to the founding of the United States, many of the inventions and services that have changed the way the human race does things have been created by this same type of personality. In every aspect of life from communication to transportation to the lighting of our buildings and homes, these Unique Renegades with a vision for something better than what we currently have were the people who drove our race forward. Many of these inventions did not have research to back them up; they were merely an IDEA in someone's imagination that came to fruition from faith and determination.

Entertainment

Many of the most successful entertainers in the world became that way from the vision or idea that was different from anyone else's. Often a story or an emotional experience in life will inspire the production of a movie or the writing of a song. It only takes a little research to understand that a large percentage of musicians, actors, and producers were and continue to be Unique Renegades inspired by what was going on in the theater of their own minds. These visions were big enough that these people felt compelled to share their idea with the world whether it was a play, movie, or music. The sphere of influence that formed around them helped see their vision to be the inspiration among the population that they had dreamed of. Dreams like this come true because many people share the same ideas and want to be entertained by them. True talent rarely has to seek an audience very long. People come from all walks of life to be that entertainer who inspires millions by BEING the part that people yearn to see.

I love these examples of the people who choose to live this way. It is easy to see what following the calling INSIDE can bring into the life of a person who has the persistence and desire to make it happen. All of these Renegades had humble beginnings and ended up being a huge influence on the world around them by discovering their TRUE inspiration.

A great example of A Unique Renegade is my son, Kenny. He has little formal education but a lot of self and technical education. He was raised with the belief that we can use our imagination to see life's future experiences. He made a point of visualizing what he wanted to do for a living daily. He studied and passed the A+ computer certification with NO formal training. The same is true for two Microsoft certifications. At 19 years old, he started a position with Lockheed Martin at the Pentagon in Washington, DC. This position required that he retain a Top Secret Clearance. He did that and was then offered another positon with the Army Corps of Engineers making almost TWICE what he did at the Lockheed Martin job. He hadn't even turned 21 yet. He has his own office. He has a luxury apartment with every amenity one could want including a deluxe gym, a theater with surround sound to watch movies, a lounge for get-togethers, retail establishments on the property and so much more. He never was told what he couldn't do. He was always encouraged about what he COULD do.

Inspired people lead inspired lives. Here are some facts that are very empowering for every single human being on this planet, including those just mentioned AND yourself:

> You are the creator of the world you live in.

> Nobody knows what is right for you except you.

> The mind is the most powerful part of the human being.

I have written this book in hopes that it will lead you to use your powerful mind in more beneficial ways. It lays the groundwork for a new belief system that will serve you very well. You can change your entire life by changing how you feel about everything in it. This book contains many resources and processes that can help you refine and control what is deep in your subconscious mind. You are ON YOUR WAY to the magnificent life you have imagined. Effectively and effortlessly master your life. Become A Unique Renegade! Enjoy the journey.

THOUGHTS ON SPIRITUALITY, RELIGION, GOVERNMENT AND "POWER"

This chapter is dedicated to offering my perspective on these subjects. This book is not written with the purpose of changing any person's religious or political beliefs. It is written to help you discover who you really are and help you better your relationship with our Creative Source. However you address this supreme power from a religious point of view is a deeply personal choice, and I appreciate that. It is my hope that this chapter brings you and I closer together so you can easily understand what is written here and start on the journey to a life you will really appreciate.

Most everyone believes there is one power that is the original Creator of All That Is. The best description I have heard for this Spirit is from Wallace D. Wattles. He states that this is the Spirit "from which all things are made and which, in its original state, permeates, penetrates, and fills the interspaces of the Universe." That is our answer to how "God is Everywhere." It also means that this is the Spirit that our Creative Source places in every one of us and allows us to use this same power to create the things and life that we want. This gives us the reason that we are "God's highest form of creation" and how we are "created in his image." He is the original Creator, and, in his image, we are creators as well. This is a power that is the greatest gift that could have ever been bestowed upon mankind. Our Creative Source "sees" all we are doing by simply being the original source for our Spirits. I like to refer to this as "The Brilliance of Infinite Perspective." At any moment, our Creative Source can see the perspective from any person at any time. Truly brilliant indeed.

Since the beginning of humanity, there have been almost as many religions as there are classes and races of people. One thing that can be said of the relationship between Spirituality and religion is that religion relies on Spirituality, and Spirituality has no dependence on religion. This is because religion is manmade, and Spirit is formless and fills all interspaces of the Universe. Spirit came first. In my mind, religion usually fails to serve humanity very well because it often tries to personify a formless Spirit in a way its followers can never fully understand. The distortions end up being huge because most of the "rules" in religion would be of no benefit to a formless Spirit of infinite intelligence. As we will see in the following "Divine, Unbreakable Law" section, there are Laws in the Universe which are always present. They set forth the responses to what we do and think continuously. Gaining an understanding of how this works is necessary on the path to becoming the Unique Renegade you want to be. As you read, maintain an open mind, and make it a point to approach this material from a deep desire of more and deeper understanding.

Government was established by man to help our race by ensuring people follow certain rules of living. Man creates what he calls "laws," but in essence, they are actually rules because rules can be broken where the natural Laws of the Universe cannot be. If we break a manmade "law," our governments reserve the right to remove us from society if someone is perceived to be too much of a danger to his fellow man. One problem with many governments is that those who are a part of the political system are assumed to be serving the people who elected them, and often they merely serve themselves. If a person is elected to a higher office, I believe that person's focus should be on the people who voted him or her into office. I also believe that there should be no such thing as "career" politicians. I think term limits should apply to every elected office there is so that fresh ideas and perspectives are always coming into the system. It is hard to grasp a person leaving their hometown to stay in Washington, DC, for example, to be a permanent part of a system that has proven to serve itself more than the people it is supposed to serve. There are people who have been in these positions for 30 or 40 years, and their constituents are some of the most underserved in the country. When you vote, consider the younger, fresh mind over the person who has been there for such a long time. Giving new ideas and points of view a chance to help change a system that many consider to be broken is a way to start things moving in a better, more positive direction.

In religion, government, and business, people tend to lust after the power of controlling others. This comes from the competitive mindset which you will read about later in the book. The competitive mindset is based on the other people or organizations losing something in order for another to meet a goal. Religion uses fear to control people. Government uses fear and "laws" that prevent people from being all they can be to control the population. The "War on Drugs" is a good example. The laws against drugs have served to create the very cartels they now have to fight. I believe all the money spent on the "War on Drugs" would be better used in a rehabilitation capacity than trying to catch every person who has an ounce or so of marijuana on them. Help the people with addictions with their behavior rather than criminalizing them and over filling our penal system with people who could contribute to society with some help.

The lust for power that so many people have is one of the biggest blocks to the development of the human mind. Those in charge of groups of people in large corporations often lead to get themselves noticed rather than leading to inspire their team. We have an understanding of the reason people chase positions of power in government. In your personal life, be the one who inspires others. You have no need to control anyone, and you should never be trying to. The human Spirit is a freedom seeking Spirit, and when it succumbs to the control of another, it loses its ability to express itself fully. In the pages of this book, we will look into many of the ways to set yourself free and express yourself to be the best, most complete person you were created to be. All in the Universe is pulling FOR you. There is nothing that wants you to do without or expand to anything less than your greatest. Get ready to learn about being the best you can and how to do this in such a way that the journey inside yourself is as amazing as it should be.

DIVINE, UNBREAKABLE LAW

What if I told you that there are laws that guide you, and you cannot break them even if you WANT TO? There are laws that have stood the test of time throughout the history of the Universe. These are laws that affect the outcome of every situation in your life. Good, bad, happy, or sad, these laws have always been a part of everything you do. You are exactly the same as all of mankind according to these Divine Laws. They are equal opportunity every time. They fill every space in the Universe. We all guide ourselves by the same laws. Dr. Warner Von Braun, the father of the space program, said: "The natural Laws of the Universe are so PRECISE that we do not have any difficulty building a space ship, sending a person to the moon and we can time the landing with the precision of a fraction of a second." Everything happens for a reason. There are no mistakes. The earth effortlessly stays in orbit around the sun. Gravity is the same every single second. No matter who you are, where you are, or what you are doing, your life's outcome is determined by the Divine Laws of the Universe, starting with the Law of Vibration.

Law of Vibration

The Law of Vibration simply states that everything is always in motion. More specifically, it says that in its most basic form, everything is light or energy which *resonates and exists as a certain frequency*. This means that things that appear solid on earth are formed from matter that, when observed with a proper (electron) microscope, is at a very high state of vibration. Absolutely everything is in some kind of motion. NOTHING rests. To understand vibration a little better, understand that it is simply represented as a frequency as illustrated below.

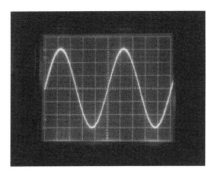

I was into electronics as a kid and used to measure electricity on different equipment. Pictured above is a sinewave on an Oscilloscope screen which represents electromagnetic waves oscillating up and down. This illustrates how vibration can be expressed as frequency. Electromagnetic waves from radio, radar, computer Wi-Fi and even the human brain produce measurable frequencies as illustrated above. The difference in these vibrations is what they are used for. The electromagnetic vibrations from our brain are used by our connected minds, bodies, and Divine Intelligence to provide this experience we call life.

Law of Polarity

This can best be described as a Law of Opposites. You can't have one without the other. It's the hot and cold, the inside and outside, the up and the down, and many other physical things which have opposing properties. The Law of Polarity, in its most basic form, is plus and minus. What this means for vibration is there are high (plus) states for vibration and low (minus) states for vibration. You can hear and feel the difference in low and high vibrations through sound. The lower vibrations give us the bass, the deep beat of the drums, and the higher vibrations give us the treble, the clash of the symbols.

Law of Attraction

This is the most popular and sometimes misunderstood of the Divine Laws. It is often taught as a primary law, but it relies on the more basic Laws of Vibration and Polarity to even exist. I like to look at it as the guide to how I am doing staying on the path to my desire. In simplest terms, the Law of Attraction states, "like attracts like." Here are some example clichés of like attracting like:

Nothing attracts a crowd like a crowd

Misery loves company

Great minds think alike

Success breeds success

So, if you are happy with what is going on in your life right now, you are going to attract more of what you are experiencing. If you don't like what is going on in your life, you are going to attract more of that as well. This is because what you are focused on and the associated feelings are sent from your brain to the Universe, and the Universe immediately responds with like vibrations. It doesn't matter if you like it or not, the Law of Attraction brings all the things you want AND don't want into your life based on what you are the most focused on. Everything you have in your life, good, bad, or otherwise, you have attracted as a result of your thought. This happens for all people regardless of whether they are aware of this or not. The wisest men in history have known this for a long time. You can go back though the history of humanity and look at every person that changed the course of human history. Every one of them understood Divine Law and used it to shape their lives and those of countless others.

VALUABLE, PRICELESS THOUGHT

Plant the seed of what you want in your mind
to get what you want out of life.

The human race has a unique gift. You and I are creators. This is because we have the ability to choose thought. This is the power of reason, as we will see in the faculties of the mind. It allows you to reject an idea if you don't like it. We also have imagination which allows us to create and hold an idea on the screen of our mind and even make it a desire if we get emotionally attached to it. This gift of creativity allows us to create the world we live in. It gives us freedom to say yes or no to any thought that comes into our awareness. Choosing thought is how we make decisions. Each person's thought is unique because everyone's perspective is unique. One can choose to share thought or use it to make their life better.

As previously mentioned, at its most basic, detectable level, thought is an electromagnetic wave like TV and radio signals. We can measure the frequency of a thought being transmitted by the brain. The difference between thought and manmade electromagnetic waves is that thought is used by the Divine Laws of the Universe to shape our lives. Every frequency has a match. When you think about something you have observed or an idea, the longer you think about it, and the stronger you feel about it, the more it attracts thoughts like itself and grows.

Nothing ever comes into being without thought being given to it first. This is why every great event and invention created in the history of humanity began as a single thought in someone's mind. The actions taken upon those thoughts have shaped the reality we live in today. As ideas emerge in the minds of people, our race will continue to evolve. We have literally thought ourselves into the reality we are in now.

This is because the mind operates much as the fertile soil of the earth does. The big difference is that the subconscious mind is FAR more fertile than even the best soil on earth. Plant an idea, and get emotionally involved with it, and that idea becomes a plant of desire that starts growing in your mind and starts its path to becoming a reality in your life. This is EXACTLY what Jesus means when he says, "As you sow, so shall you reap." Inanimate thoughts are the seeds for all creation. God made us all creators, his highest form of creation, for a reason. He wants to create with and through us. What an awesome privilege it is to work with the Creator of All That Is to make your own desires happen.

Generally speaking, there are two ways of thinking that humanity follows. One is to think based on what you observe. This is thinking by default. You observe something and act on your observation. There is also inspired thought. This is the light bulb moment. The "I have a great idea" moment. You feel strong motivation to follow this idea to its fruition. This is where every single great change in humanity has emanated from. All inspiring inventions, creations, circumstances and experiences come from ideas which evolve from inspired thought. Every thought offered is eternal and, therefore, shapes eternity. As we create on earth, we create in eternity as well. Do you like your contribution to eternity? If not, is now not a good time to improve the ideas you are offering?

I also appreciate The Brilliance of Infinite Perspective that our Creative Source has....being able to understand every belief, concern, or desire of every person on this planet and respond with perfection every time, no exceptions. Every time you send a thought, a wish, or a prayer (which is usually a thought expressed in words), our Source responds with a vibration which is an essence of the feeling in that thought. So, make sure that as you pray, you are visualizing and feeling that which you wish to see happening. You are more likely to get the response you want that way.

Make sure that you don't demand answers from a point of feeling bad about something. That feeling will end up being your prayer. Instead, ask for inspired ideas. Inspired thought is always a Divine gift. It opens up new avenues on your journey. Inspired people are happy people. Happy people attract happy people. Demanding people are the same way, attracting demanding people. Inspire yourself.

Given that everything good begins as thought, imagine something that will make you feel really good as if you already have it. Think of how the others around you will benefit simply from your feeling good. Always keep in mind that what you are feeling about something is feedback in the form of thought that you are sharing with the Universe as well. Allow yourself the luxury of saying yes to your own desire. You deserve it. Now just do it.

Remember thoughts that DO NOT serve us well work the same way. The mind is just as receptive to a "bad" thought as a "good" thought. Bringing a thought to fruition is a lot like raising a plant. A good example is that you can plant food or poison, and the soil of the earth will return both in equal abundance. The subconscious mind is FAR more fertile than even the earth. Be clear on the thoughts you plant in your mind. Make sure that when you get what you think about (and you WILL), it is indeed what you want. Remember, "As you sow, so you shall reap." Yes, this is an illustration that likens what you plant in the earth to what you plant in your mind.

All of us should appreciate and use the creative power of thought to its fullest. The human experience is enriched when people give thought to something that inspires them. We then get the creations and ideas that benefit all. Humanity as a whole feels better. And our race continues to evolve closer to its full potential.

UNDERSTANDING YOUR OWN MIND

The mind is the most powerful thing a human being possesses. At the same time, it is the most underutilized part of most human beings. The subconscious mind is incalculably powerful when it is focused on a clear vision or desire. Remember the illustration regarding the soil and the mind. The subconscious mind is FAR more fertile than the best soil on earth. We already understand what Jesus meant when he said, "As ye sow, so shall ye reap." When we plant an idea there, and nurture it like in a garden, the result is what we planted in our mind becoming reality. The other side of this is when you plant a seed of thought that you don't want; that begins to be what you reap as well. Spend lots of time placing what you are inspired by in your mind.

This can be done through a process Napoleon Hill calls "auto-suggestion." What auto-suggestion will do is plant a message for a goal or desire in your subconscious mind. To make things clearer, it is important to understand that you have a conscious and a subconscious mind, and they have very different functions.

The mind can best be illustrated as Dr. Thurman Fleet did back in the 1930s. The illustration (page 32) illustrates the mind's relationship with the body.

As we can see, the top part of the mind is the conscious mind, and the bottom part of the mind that interfaces with the body and produces the results we see in life is known as the subconscious mind. You will notice in the picture that the subconscious mind is connected to the body. The way this works is that your subconscious mind has a "program" that basically runs your life on a daily basis. All of your habits, those you appreciate and all the others, reside in the subconscious mind. This is where auto-suggestion

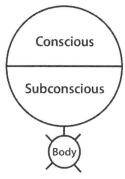

comes into play. Napoleon Hill wrote about this in *Think and Grow Rich*. He said, "Through the dominating thoughts which one permits to remain in the conscious mind (whether these thoughts are negative or positive is immaterial), the principle of auto-suggestion voluntarily reaches the subconscious mind and influences it with these thoughts." As an example, let's say you want another hour in the day to get more done toward your dream. Your habits have you accustomed to getting out of bed at 7:30 am. You could set the alarm earlier, but there is a high likelihood you would fall back into the habit of waking up at 7:30 am through the snooze button or setting the alarm back. A more effective way is to repeat to yourself at night, every night, what you are going to do when you wake up at 6:30 am. "My intention is to wake up at 6:30 am. I will immediately study and then take a walk with the extra hour." This is auto-suggestion and, through repetition, will begin to influence the subconscious mind. Do this for 30 days, and you will likely have a new default awakening time. Work on changing one or two habits at a time to begin the process of changing the "program" that runs you.

Success comes from programming the subconscious mind for success. Success is the fulfillment of one's desires. Success is happiness in the journey of life. Success, therefore, is not typical or normal. It IS an attitude one carries which expands the Spirit and creates the desire of wanting MORE of what is being experienced in life. Remember that human life, like nature, is for the *fuller* expression of everything we desire. All evidence in nature and the Universe shows us that this is true. If you want more of what you are living, you are successful. Your mind is programmed to lead you to a life that is very fulfilling. If you wish for something different, you have to align with that desire to allow it to become reality. This requires programming your subconscious mind to perform the actions that lead to the life you want. Visualization and belief in that visualization is the fastest path to this programming and, thus, your desire. Impressing what you want on your subconscious mind through constant, spaced repetitions of visualizations of the result you want will lead to success. You don't need or want anyone to tell you how to do it. You only have to have the vision and the will to follow it to fruition in order to create the reality.

Mindset

This brings us to mindset. The right mindset is *critical* to moving an idea into the subconscious mind successfully. The mind has two high level perspectives it functions from. They are the competitive mind and the creative mind. These are opposing mindsets and have differing outcomes.

The competitive mindset operates by comparing current, existing ideas and circumstances for merit or lack thereof. This puts someone or others at a disadvantage by assuming that one party or more has to lose. In a Universe with an infinite supply of the energy required to make *anything happen*, this is never a true assumption. The competitive mind works from what already is, assumes there are limitations and tries to make the case that what it believes is better for anyone involved. It tries to reduce ideas of others to having less value than its own. From this the beliefs of superiority and inferiority are born. The idea that prevails is supposedly the winner, but at what cost? Other ideas which don't find their ideal circumstance? Less than fuller expansion of those who think differently? One who believes that he or she thrives on competition is always looking to be "better than" another. They limit their minds to comparison versus using their imagination. They are always trying to "one up" the other guy. The competitive mindset is a losing proposition for all involved since it assumes a person or idea has to be less than another.

The creative mind functions exactly as Divine Spirit does. It is always seeking fuller expression and gets its ideas from inspired thought which is originated by its owner or Divine Source. This is the mindset that is responsible for every great idea since mankind began. Everything from the car to the internet to all of the technology we enjoy today began as a single, inspired thought in a creative mind and was nurtured to grow from its beginning through fruition. The competitive mindset did not even play into these ideas as they were original, unique ideas. There is no competition. There was just this life altering idea moving into reality. The true professional operates from the creative mindset. This person or group of people always employ the imagination and deep reasoning to come up with truly life-changing, innovative ideas. There is never a concern about competition because they know from the power of their minds the next amazing idea is right around the corner.

It is important to understand that in a world where there is so much competition, the phrase Bob Proctor uses, "Amateurs compete. Professionals create." can be proven repeatedly. It is always the people with the creative mindset that find success, prosperity, and wealth very easily. True, Unique Renegades do not have to compete to have their desires fulfilled. They simply follow their own inspired thought to their own bliss. Finding your bliss does not require competition, but it does require your utmost best in offering your creative gifts to the world around you.

Another thing to consider regarding keeping a strong, creative mindset is not to base any part of your life on "they or that person might think I am dumb." Any sentence, with a good or bad message, and the words "I am" in it, is incredibly powerful. In this case, we have the "I am dumb." in the sentence. This is literally verbal abuse of yourself. You would NEVER deliberately abuse others like that, so why leave yourself to this self-torture? Combining this thought with the power of the emotion of worry, you can start to feel a little less intelligent over time. Also, observe the people whom you think might belittle you if you ask for better under-standing on a certain subject. That person is likely of the competitive mind and feels like he must belittle others to make him- or herself feel important. So, don't give a second thought to what this person thinks of your quest for understanding because 1) It is none of your business what they think, and 2) It is none of their business WHY you are seeking this understanding unless you share it with them. THE most important opinion of you is YOUR OWN. Keep that in mind, and "let the haters compete and hate." You continue to *create* for yourself. Doing so will have the effect of improving the lives of those around you from the inspiration they draw from watching you grow creation by creation. What a great way to be.

Evolving from the Competitive to the Creative Mindset

The creative person understands at a very deep level that his or her prosperity does not have to come from someone or some entity losing something so they can gain. The creative person knows beyond a shadow of a doubt that there is an infinite source of supply for everything that has ever been created in the history of the Universe. Moving from the competitive mindset to the creative one involves removing any thoughts of limits preventing success in their life. The Universe at large has always been expanding with no evidence of disintegration at any time in this history. The Universe and all of life on earth are always for fuller expression of life. Remember that any idea that has moved to the point of being a subconscious desire is seeking fuller expression through that person. The person who is living with a competitive mindset finds reasons and ways to limit his or her belief of what can even become a desire. These people think desire is a "sin" and that their Divine Creator that they refer to as God sees desire as wrong. Since every particle of the Universe is always for more expression, one must begin to understand a little more every day that this is THE nature of ALL things in the Universe. As living beings, we are either creating or disintegrating. Creating is living; disintegrating is dying. You are here to live and become the fullest expression of yourself that you possibly can. This means that every worthy ideal you are moving toward is a fuller expression of your Spirit seeking to come to the surface.

The Six Faculties of the Conscious Mind

The human mind has six faculties that should be considered the muscles of the mind. They are imagination, reason, memory, perception, will and intuition.

Imagination is the most amazing faculty that the human mind possesses and is what sets us apart from the rest of the animal kingdom as our Creator's HIGHEST form of creation. We can use the imagination to come up with a new idea, picture what things will be like when our ideas are reality, build and improve things to the way we want them to be and so much more. Albert Einstein was a huge proponent of imagination in his writings. One of his most important quotes on the subject was this: "Imagination is more important than knowledge. For knowledge is limited, whereas imagination embraces the entire world, stimulating progress, giving birth to evolution." Giving birth to evolution. How awesome is that? Give birth to the full evolution of your ideas, and change the world you are creating in a WONDERFUL way. Be grateful for your imagination by using it on a daily basis.

Reason is the ability to think. We can choose thoughts and accept or reject ideas using this faculty. The majority of people don't use their reason effectively and end up with subconscious beliefs and habits they would rather not have. When something you are reasoning with does not align with what you really desire in your life, REJECT it! We have that ability as our Creator's HIGHEST form of creation. Use your reasoning faculty to pass marvelous images to your other faculties, including the imagination, to allow yourself to fall in love with the ideas that will make your life better.

Memory is the ability to remember ideas, circumstances, and events in our lives. We often hear people talk about a bad memory, but remember that memory is a *mental muscle* that can be developed with the right exercises. Those exercises are outside the scope of this book, but there are many that can help develop a superior memory. A good, developed memory is a great way to hold onto ideas we want to develop an emotional, subconscious attachment to. The better and more developed your memory is, the easier it is to recall pictures and facts for the other faculties of the mind to work with.

Perception is the unique point of view any of us develops for a subject, event, circumstance or idea that may have multiple points of view by many. Think of how a light shines on something and produces a shadow on the other side. The angle that the light is shining at is similar to your perception of a subject. It is the "angle" you see it at. You may think an idea isn't for you, and the next person may be really inspired by the same idea. Remember that both perceptions are important and are of tremendous value because they cause us to perceive the differences in everything around us and choose and appreciate what will make life better for us.

Will gives us the ability to focus on only one thing to the exclusion of everything else. When the will is used in conjunction with the imagination, we can take a single idea and keep it on the screen of our mind long enough to get emotionally attached to it. As we do that, this wonderful idea gets further and further impressed on the subconscious mind. Use your will often to keep your dream in the forefront of your thoughts and in your imagination at the exclusion of everything else. A great way to exercise the will is to find something simple, a picture or a small light, to focus on for a set amount of time. As you practice this, the amount of time you are focusing on this object will grow longer and longer, and you can practice holding your mind to more and more subjects to the exclusion of others. You'll benefit greatly from this exercise.

Intuition is defined as "the power or faculty of attaining direct knowledge or cognition without evident rational thought and inference." What this illustrates is the light bulb moment. The inspired idea which comes to one without having to use reason or originate an idea. This is when an idea for something just "comes" to you, and it has an immediate, inspiring impact. These are the ideas you want to get emotionally involved with. You want to use the combined power of your will and imagination to bring this idea into reality for the good of yourself and all around you. Think of the automobile. The computer operating systems that gave us the personal computer and smartphones. Facebook and social media. These all were very unique ideas likely inspired by an intuitive thought and brought into reality through the will and imagination of the mind.

Develop these faculties, and use them to hone your personality for your own benefit. Never try to be like others want you to be because they cannot possibly know what is best for you, nor can they inspire you as your own well-developed mind can. You can't copy or imitate someone else's idea nearly as effectively as you can see your own to fruition. No one has ever copy-catted themselves into true prosperity. Only you can understand what is the most inspiring and best for you. Throw away the personality aspects that don't serve you regardless of who or where they came from. If they are subconscious habits, develop your mind by finding habits that serve you to replace them. Set time aside to practice those habits daily until they become routine. Alignment with your authentic self is the fastest path to the fulfillment of what you want to live. Be less like others and more like yourself. You have more to offer the world as yourself than anyone else.

If what you have your mind on is something you don't like, get your mind on something better. Plant a new seed. As we focus on our thoughts, they become stronger and bring their essence into our life. Always focus on what you want, even if "what is" is not something you want. Get the essence of what you want by putting the majority of your focus on only that. It works. There is living proof all around you.

EDUCATION, UNDERSTANDING, AND KNOWLEDGE

"When the student is ready, the teacher will appear."
~Buddha

The word education has Latin roots: from *ē* ("from, out of") and *dūcō* ("I lead, I conduct"). As we see, it can mean "I lead from or out of." There are many places to find education. Most "education" can really be defined more as indoctrination as most public institutions show their students how to memorize facts or processes and then repeat them from memory in return for a favorable grade. As we have begun to study the mind in the previous chapter, you see that while this can equip the conscious mind with knowledge of skills, it teaches nothing in terms of earning an income or awareness of prosperity and success. None of this is taught in any schools from the early years clear up until college. The idea of an imagined thought becoming what is imagined by the creative thinker is often called a "pipe dream" and not possible to create. What I love about the creative side of society is that the most creative ideas, inventions, and things that we use today were merely a tiny thought in someone's mind in their infancy. Just think about what would have happened if Thomas Edison gave up on the light bulb or Alexander Graham Bell never made a telephone that worked.

Keeping the mind in the classroom all the time, and never feeding it from the outside world, leaves it with unfulfilled desire. I think the late Stella Adler said it best when she said, "You cannot afford to confine your studies to the classroom. The Universe and all of history is your classroom." There are so many sources of information and levels of learning and understanding. There are personal experiences, challenges, new ideas, mentors and so much more. To believe that a diploma or degree from a public institution equips its students to be the successful, prosperous human beings they inspire to be is foolish. There are many people who have multiple degrees on their business cards, and the difference between the knowledge they have and the amount of this knowledge that they ever even try to use for ANYONE's benefit is tremendous. Taking your understanding and applying it to what the world needs gives your educated mind value that you can offer to people or corporations.

Keep in mind that you learn more when you are inspired to learn the way you want to. You learn little, if anything, when you learn the way you are told to learn. You will find that the application of a subject you appreciate comes much easier than something you were "required" to learn. Make sure your learning is inspired from the voice inside. Let all of the others attempt to understand that noise outside.

Some of today's school systems use a system called "Common Core." If this is really common, I'll take uncommon. Yes 2+2 always equals 4, but those are basic facts. Once thinking via imagination comes into play, public schools tend to discourage that. You get the "Johnny, pay attention!" syndrome. Common Core just stymies teachers by saying you have to hit your numbers. It has nothing to do with stimulating imagination or inspiring new understanding. Common Core goes after knowledge standards proven by metrics. Meeting these types of objectives does not expand the mind. It says you must follow the rules. Teaching by inspiring understanding opens the mind and fosters creativity. Backing a kid into a corner, as in this example, does not help him or her in any way, fashion, or form. It can be considered a risk to place a child in the public school system these days. Too much indoctrination and not enough feeding of the young, fertile mind. It does not exercise the imagination and, in fact, discourages it.

Let's imagine a good alternative to the current system. Little eight-year-old Johnny is in a class being taught science. His mind drifts off and imagines a unique electric bike which would take him farther than his current, self-powered bike. Today, as the teacher's curriculum is the most important thing to him or her in this moment, he or she would likely say, "Pay attention, Johnny!" Poof. End of imagined creation in action. Maybe it would be better if the teacher walked up to Johnny and asked, "What are you thinking?" Little Johnny says, "I'm dreaming of an electric bike to ride to school." The teacher says, "Can you draw that for me, Johnny?" He does and has all the details in the drawing. The battery, the motor, the drive belt for moving the bike. He tells the teacher, "It is rechargeable, too." Tell me, which is the better learning experience?

If you have children, ensure that they are encouraged, if not required, to develop their imagination daily. Do what you can to make sure their teachers also understand the value of imagination. It is this faculty of the mind that produces all of the best inventions, circumstances, and events throughout the course of humanity. It stands to reason then that the young adult with a very fertile imagination will go far in the world. He or she will be using the creative mind to create things that inspire others. They will be THE most valuable in their chosen fields. Hyphenate the word. Imagine-Nation. Send your kids to the Imagine-Nation often. As Albert Einstein said, "Imagination is everything. It is the preview of life's coming attractions."

Understanding

True understanding is the power of comprehension. Knowledge is awareness. Understanding occurs at a far deeper level than knowledge does. This is not to say that knowledge does not have value. It does. But you have to add study to knowledge to get understanding. I am sure you can see that studying that which you are aware of creates better understanding. I encourage you to consider these two statements, and ask yourself which is more believable. One is, "I know what is going on here." Two is, "I understand what is going on here." Which statement has more power? Which is more convincing? Knowing something means being aware of it; understanding means having a detailed comprehension of the subject. Something you could easily impart to another.

As Napoleon Hill wrote, "An educated man is not, necessarily, one who has an abundance of general or specialized knowledge. An educated man is one who has so developed the faculties of his mind that he may acquire anything he wants, or its equivalent, without violating the rights of others." This mindset comes from true understanding, not programmed or memorized knowledge. The fact is that in relative terms, knowledge is cheap, and understanding is priceless. Gaining a full understanding of the relationship between money and success is vital to true prosperity.

Knowledge is a building block of understanding. Knowing the answer to a math equation is a part of understanding how to arrive at the correct answer. Going through the process of working a formula with no aids to get the correct answer demonstrates understanding. This means you can derive the information you need because you have done the same process over and over. This goes beyond simple memorization. It is rooted in your subconscious mind.

The best way to become truly educated?

Study every day. Make it a point to understand your subject. Make it a point to understand yourself. Go out and experience anything you can. Build on that idea that inspires you. Use history and the Universe to research and obtain understanding of the details. Get a mentor who has great experience and understanding of the subject you are studying. Make sure it is clear to you that you don't fully understand something unless you can lead someone else, too. As you understand more subjects, you will better understand yourself, your life, and be much more aligned with the success and prosperity you seek. One of the qualities of a true Renegade is that they understand themselves and their goals better than anyone else. They use this understanding to change the world around them which always changes the world of MANY others in a very positive way.

Develop your imagination. Like any muscle group, imagination will improve with constant use. As a rule, school curriculum focuses very little, if at all, on the imagination. But, as Albert Einstein famously said, "The true sign of intelligence is not knowledge but imagination." As we have seen and will see all through this book, the power of an imagined idea is infinite. When the human imagination is used to its full potential, life-changing ideas and inventions are brought into our reality. Imagination started the creation of the wheel, automobile, internet and smartphones. Keep your mind fertile. Use your imagination to come up with ideas that can make your life better at work or at home. Who knows? YOU may have the next BIG idea. Make sure it has a well-developed mind to grow in.

Speaking of the mind, make sure yours is open. Open-minded people, by their very nature, are open to being inspired by that new idea because the thoughts they think are aligned with the inspired thought that can be nurtured into the next big thing. A good example of keeping an open mind is this anonymous quote: "Don't tell me the sky is the limit when there are footprints on the moon." Embrace all possibilities. Many things we take for granted today seemed impossible when they were only ideas. The light bulb, automobile, television, radio, telephone and computers were all hatched from a single thought in someone's mind. Never underestimate the power of desire blended with faith through understanding. Because of the right open-minded people and imagination, we have things in our world that were never even dreamed of before. It's a wonderful time to be alive.

EMOTIONS: YOUR SUBCONSCIOUS IS TALKING TO YOU!

"There is a voice that doesn't use words. Listen."
~ Rumi

How many times do you feel like saying, "If I only had known." What happens in so many of these cases is that a voice was trying to inform you, and you were NOT tuned in. Our emotions are our subconscious or higher-self speaking to us. When you are in an emotional high, the message is that you are on track on your journey. You are focused on what will bring out fuller expression of your life. When you feel not so good, you are off track. Remember that the subconscious mind is the emotional mind, and its response to any thought is your emotional reaction to that thought. The message is simple: either think a new thought to get back on track, or bring yourself into emotional appreciation of this new reality you have somehow found yourself in. People often feel off when they are taking a new risk or a chance at the unfamiliar. Through understanding of this new subject or reality, you can find your way back into a very positive feeling. Let's study and better understand the emotions below:

Belief

Belief happens when you repeat an idea constantly to yourself, and it becomes a subconscious thought. At a subconscious level, beliefs deeply impressed on our subconscious minds control every aspect of the life we are living. As we have also learned, a habit is a belief we impress on the subconscious mind by practicing it over and over. Beliefs can affirm what we consider to be good. Our belief system is essential to helping us find the good around us.

Many beliefs serve us well. They serve to motivate us and help us achieve goals. They can provide a strong sense of wellbeing when they are empowering thoughts. Others can stop people from ever achieving anything when they are disempowering. A good example is terrorists. They are taught that people who believe differently from them will harm them. They live life disempowered from a very early age. Many of them think that if they take enough lives, they will be rewarded. Truly empowered people never have to take anything from others. They know that wellbeing is natural and pursue it. Your beliefs are strong influences on the outcome of your life. They produce the results that you see day by day.

Every belief began as a single thought. This thought could have come from exposure to it or inspiration. The ideas that will inspire you the most come from inside. Many of them came from intuition. It's easy to read something and get inspired, but it is far more rewarding to think of something that leaves you inspired. True inspiration that can change your life always comes from within.

Belief is the result of successful auto-suggestion in action. Understand that whatever you are doing in your life is as important and worthy as you believe it is. No one else is creating your reality; you are. No one's opinion about your current circumstance matters unless you make it an issue. It truly is none of your business. Understand that your life is what you have made it up 'til now. The only thing that will change it is a change in your beliefs and what you choose to pay attention to. Pay attention to what makes you feel better, and you will feel better. Conversely, pay attention to what you perceive as problems, and they will grow. Love yourself enough to pay attention to what you REALLY want. Leave the other stuff to diminish in your greatness. You know life is grand. Live like it is.

Desire

When you want something, the emotion expressed is desire. Wallace Wattles wrote: "Desire is possibility seeking expression, or function seeking performance." Once a want is impressed on the subconscious mind enough, it will begin to be expressed as desire. You can have desire for things such as relationships, materials, or knowledge. When desire is expressed, it starts to invoke the Law of Attraction through the increased and repetitive attention given to it. If you see the image of what you want, you want to impress it on your subconscious mind, feel good about that image, and get emotionally invested in it. At this point, the Law of Attraction will begin to work to make it so. You now have a desire in your subconscious mind. You can then have feelings of hope and even passion as your path leads you to this desire. The key here is to never stop believing you can have it. This is where listening to the pure desire that exists inside you (what you want to do) versus listening to what is outside you (all of the voices and noise from the world telling you what you are supposed to do) is so important. If you want it, feel like you deserve it, and can really feel what it is like to have it, you can be the Unique Renegade you WANT to be.

Hope

Hope is that feeling you have when you bring about an idea or desire in your conscious mind and then wish for and want it enough that you begin to impress it on your subconscious mind. All of us have thought, "I hope this happens or comes or becomes." It is the feeling after you have "asked the Universe" to bring something into your life and are patiently waiting for it to come. Remember, it is not the words that are being heard; it is your thoughts and the feelings from them. Hope is an excellent way to get the creative process rolling in your life. It can move the imaginary process forward by allowing you to feel what it will be like when you receive what you want. Always act on hope. Do what you can to create the feeling of the idea or desire already present in your life. Hold on to that feeling, and allow it to grow. This will keep the creative process bringing very good things into your life.

Faith

Faith is a form of strong, personal belief. The important thing to understand is that there are two forms of faith. Faith through understanding is effective, and blind faith is weak. Faith through understanding is incredibly strong. Clarence Smithison wrote on this type of faith saying: "Faith is the ability to see the invisible, to believe in the incredible, and that will permit us to receive what the masses call impossible." It literally dissolves fear and other barriers to the fulfillment of dreams. It says that you have studied that which you seek and fully understand the positive impact it can have on yourself and others. It fully empowers you to take that journey into the unknown. It gives you the strength you need to persevere in the face of adversity. Faith through understanding paves the road to success. Blind faith isn't worth the space I am using to write about it. It is a weak, slightly hopeful idea based on believing that what someone else said or wrote will change something in a meaningful way. The first bump in your journey down this road, and you are in the ditches. Avoid blind faith at all costs. Be aware that faith through understanding creates self-empowered people. As you take an idea from its first stages to something that you are emotionally invested in within your subconscious mind, it becomes easy to recall and feel very good about this idea. A self-empowered person knows that their power comes from within and uses that power for their own higher good and the higher good of people around them. These are the difference makers in our society. Their faith comes from the Divine power that gives them life. They don't want or need to give their power to anyone or anything else because they do the most good with their own power.

Passion

Passion is a strong or extravagant fondness, enthusiasm, or desire for something in life. It fuels creativity through the use of imagination and is the vehicle from which many of life's conveniences came from. In the early 90s when personal computers were just becoming popular, Bill Gates stated that he had a vision of a computer in every home. That vision has come true in the sense that the vast majority of people who want a computer have one. And most of these computers run Microsoft® Windows. This is quite a statement for what passion combined with very clear vision can accomplish. Henry Ford had a passion for horseless transportation. These men attracted things that changed the world by virtue of their strong, positive feeling about what they wanted. When we combine our vision with passion and strong positive feelings about something, the end result is always good. Think about this again: everything great that has happened since the beginning of mankind began as a single thought in someone's mind. The human mind has shaped the destiny of mankind since the beginning. There are absolutely no accidents. Everyone has the same potential. An idea in your mind may well be the next revolution in society.

Appreciation

Appreciation for what is good in your life is something you must express on a daily basis. Once you know what you want, look around. There are things, events, and relationships in your life that you can feel very thankful for. And you should! This feeling of appreciating your current moment is very positive and connects with the positive forces of the Universe. So, tune out completely what you don't want, and be very glad for what you have and what you have to look forward to. This is the life that you have created, and you have brought things into your life that are worthy of you. Feel how good it is to know that things are going to get even better by the use of your own mind. Everyone has created good things in their life. Focus on your own good events, circumstances, and creations. Give as much thanks as you can. A wonderful exercise is to write down ten things you appreciate each day. This is another way of guiding your thoughts so that there is not time for the negative thoughts to form in your mind. The more you master the feeling of your thoughts, the more control of your life you have.

Fear

Fear is also a form of strong, personal belief. Many people mistake fear for faith. This happens when people believe in things that they know are untrue at a deep, emotional level. Examples are other people's ideas of right and wrong, religions and political parties. They allow these fears to limit their potential without understanding the real power that exists inside them. They are led to believe that it is wrong to live the life of wellbeing that everyone deserves. Fear also becomes disempowering when we believe an outcome will be one we don't like and, therefore, do not even try to succeed at something. Fear isn't always disempowering. All of us remember touching something that was too hot at some point in our lives. An immediate fear of burns results because we never want to feel that pain again.

Remember that fear prevents a lot of great people from reaching their full potential. Fear begins to slow your pursuit of wellbeing when you let it limit your full potential. The fears of not knowing how, not succeeding in a challenging situation, or being rejected are common day fears people have. When dealing with fears of this nature, see the fear as a path to your full potential. Follow that path. Be positive. "I can do this." If you fear not knowing how, research what the end result needs to be. Gain clear understanding. Remember the power of faith through understanding. If the end result requires something you don't understand, research it, and get every resource you can to help you learn how. You will always be a better person when you have learned and fully understood something useful. If you fear the challenge of a situation, place an image of yourself in your mind of having conquered that challenge. Relish the feeling. Hold on to that feeling. Make that the end result in your mind. Not the challenge itself but the mastering of your own fear to conquer that challenge. Now, the subconscious sees your image of this challenge, and the Universe will be on your side. You are attracting success. The Universe is a nice teammate to have on your side. If your fear is one of rejection, make your request or situation known with the outcome you want in mind. Think and feel as if your request is already accepted. If the answer is not your expectation, the Universe has heard your feelings on the subject and is arranging an experience related to what you wanted for your life. So, today's answer may be no, but the feeling you are carrying along with your thought aligns with the answer yes from the Universe. It will happen. And when it does, you will be dazzled and amazed by what is delivered. Following the path of your fear to success as a habit will make you a free person in the long run. If you live on the edge of your fear, if you know your limits without question, you will be very happy with how people and the world receive you.

Worry

Worry is the act of using the mind to turn an idea we don't like into a fear, or worse, reality. When someone "worries" about what will happen, they have an idea in their conscious mind that something bad is going to happen. Now, we have a seed. They keep thinking the thought over and over. They are planting the seed. If they cultivate this enough, they are in danger of inviting it into their reality, *WANTED OR NOT!* The polar opposite to worry is faith through understanding. Understand that the outcome you desire is literally your birthright. Don't invest any time in the emotion of worry. Think about what you *DO WANT*, get excited about it, and commence that journey.

Guilt

Guilt is an emotion that empowers the most manipulative people in your life. If you don't believe it, look closer at the people around you. When someone uses your emotions to get you to think the way they want you to, particularly on controversial issues, they use guilt. Think about buying a car for example. You come in ready to pay the fairest price you can for "the car. You make your offer, it comes back high, you say no, and the salesman points out how he needs this sale to put food on the table. He shows you the picture of his wife and kid(s) and attempts to get you "just a few hundred" higher on the price. The best approach to this one? Tell him to take your price so he can get to the next sale. He can put food on the table faster that way. In the world of politics, guilt is used to persuade people to pay higher taxes because they are wealthy. These extra tax dollars will help the needy and trim the deficit. A better way to help the needy might be for the community around them to make them productive in society. Politicians can trim the deficit by living within the means of the yearly tax income just as they expect the population to live within the means of their household income. Do not let people manipulate you with guilt. When you become wealthy, understand that your wealth came from the Divine Power of the Universe and your work. Never feel guilty about living in abundance. You have every right to enjoy anything you desire.

Jealousy

An attitude of jealousy is one of the most destructive there can be. The Divine Laws of the Universe are not based on your changing other people's reality. The Universe has an unlimited supply of wellbeing. The proof is in the feeling every time you are jealous. Remember, the thought or action, the feeling from the thought or action, and what comes into your life will match every time. So, if you are jealous of your neighbors' car, you have the feeling of jealousy along with the desire for that exact car. The feeling that comes from this thought will produce a match. Since you don't want your neighbor to have the car because you feel as though you deserve it, the car becomes a stronger match for your neighbor. Recall that what you don't want is also arranged into your life experience. Now, recall that when you want something, and the feeling is positive, you have a good match for what will become. Get to the dealer, find the car for you, get into the feeling place deep inside that you have that car, and it is well on its way to becoming a part of your life. It is important to believe you can have it without being a burden on anyone else including yourself and your family. Believe and feel that you deserve it. This is very powerful because you are using the Law of Attraction to allow the Universe to provide what you want. The stronger the joy that comes from your thoughts is, the better the match. Find the desires that you want. Do not think about what other people have. In fact, compliment them on it. Do this knowing and feeling that the right match for you will flow into your life simply by feeling good and intending to have it. This serves you and your fellow man far better than jealousy.

Anger

Anger is such a self-destructive emotion, yet most people have the ability to change their reactions to most of the situations which make them angry. The next time you feel anger, try to imagine how you appear to the world around you. When you feel angry, acknowledge it to yourself. Do not try to hide it or justify it. Recognize it. Look at the event and emotion that caused the anger. If it was out of love and protective, like if your child is getting into something that could harm him or her, then follow the anger through to its resolution. Guide your thoughts of this moment so that the path that led to this anger from love leads you back into only love. Make sure every-one involved knows you still love and care for them. If the anger is from a situation that you simply don't like or find distasteful, stop and feel the moment. If your anger is making the situation worse, remove yourself from it if possible. If that is not possible, do your best to take the emotion out of the situation. Be aware of the things that are going well in your life, and put your focus on them. A simple shift in awareness can make many situations much easier to handle. Inconsiderate people and life's unpleasant, little events are all around you. Guiding your thoughts to allow the best outcome of any situation will bring more positive events into your life. The more positive events that enter your life, the less room there is for the negative events. Forgive and forget is important here. The less you focus on how someone or some business "wronged" you, the more you can follow the path to your own abundance. If you are happy, who cares what they think about you?

As we can see, it is clear that the effects of our emotions on our lives are never ending. They produce feelings that create the beliefs we hold. Our strong beliefs manifest themselves in the form of faith or fear. We are at our strongest when our beliefs are empowering and at our weakest when our fears or worries are disempowering. Reaching for thoughts that empower us is highly beneficial to the human race both individually and as a whole.

ALIGNING WITH WHAT YOU WANT

Start with gratitude. Showing joy, appreciation, or love for what you already have is the most important step in bringing any new goal or desire into your life. Think of gratitude as your relationship with your Creator. A large number of people only show gratitude at a specific time or as a religious ritual on a certain day. They then leave their Creator out of the picture for the rest of the week. What I have personally found is that this is a relationship that is very much worth nurturing on a moment by moment basis. As you move closer to God in gratitude, He and all you are asking for move closer to you. Give and you will receive. This definitely applies to gratitude. Be happy for what you have, and more of what you truly appreciate will come your way. Our Creator is formless and permeates all areas of the Universe. Any thought you offer begins to move into form shortly after you offer the thought. Make sure you are offering thoughts of gratitude for what exists now AND what is coming. As you become more appreciative of what you are imagining as if you already have it, it is being drawn closer to you. Any time spent dwelling on what you do not want draws that closer, too. Make it a part of your habitual thought process to be glad for all that you have in your mind and in your life right now.

Recall that your emotions are the results of thoughts that you are thinking right now. That's because your subconscious mind has an "opinion" of what you are thinking about. You interpret that "opinion" as feeling or emotion. So, whatever it is you are thinking about, if the feeling coming from the thought is not aligned with how you want to feel, there are two simple choices. The first way is to align with the subject that you are thinking about. Write down the positive aspects of this subject, and start to get invested in it emotionally if it is a new idea, want, or goal you are working on. Work on moving it into the space in your emotions where you really feel appreciation about seeing it manifest in your life. If you do this right, it will go from feeling uncomfortable to being a desire in your subconscious mind. Then all you must do is act on thought inspired by this desire to bring it forth into your life. The second way is simpler if the thought is just something you don't want. Use reason to reject the current thought. You want to keep your mind on your dreams, desires, and goals. These are the thoughts and imagined ideas that you appreciate. Appreciating anything is showing gratitude.

Think of getting in the feeling place of appreciation as the BEST way to show gratitude to the Divine Source of life. Remember that what you are putting out COMES BACK, and we want all that comes back to fall into that category that we appreciate. The aspects of what you are paying attention to will dictate the mood you are in by your emotional relationship with them, so do your best to keep your attention on that which generates the deep feeling of appreciation in you. Always strive to be working from the best feeling possible. With practice this can become your default mode of operation, and you will find the things flowing to you from your journey to be very satisfying and worthy of you.

Now, determine what you want. Be very clear on the what. You want as much detail as possible. This has to be something you can get emotionally involved with. It might be a position in life, a large goal that you have never accomplished before, a home, a mate or any number of things that would make you happy with them in your reality. The reason people want anything in their lives is because they believe they will feel better when they have it.

It is important not to have your desire stem from jealousy. As we discovered in the chapter on emotions, jealousy just makes whatever you are jealous of a stronger match to the owner. An example is that you see that red BMW convertible in your neighbor's driveway. Well, get to the dealers, and look at some convertibles yourself. You might find a Mercedes favorable over the BMW. Now, you have made a decision on something easy to fall in love with because YOU chose it.

Ask yourself why you want it. Is this to fill a void or empty space in your life? Is it a goal you want to accomplish because of its chance of improving your world and the world of those around you? Is it a solution? The why will help you get emotionally invested in it and move it into the subconscious mind as a desire. We want our wants to become desires in order to engage the Divine Power of the Heavens. So, give your wants and ideas all of the personal justification you can muster by answering why to get involved with them. Again, remember that writing about your wants and desires is VERY powerful. They are the children of your mind. Nurture them as attentively as you would a child.

Another way of getting on the path to what you want is visualizing. See what you want on the screen of your mind. Make this an exercise you practice every day more than once. The reason is that we want to impress this on our subconscious mind so that Divine forces come together to lead us in the path of our desires. Let's review what Wallace Wattles wrote: "Desire is possibility seeking expression, or function seeking performance." Once your want is impressed on your subconscious mind, it is expressed as desire. Every time you imagine it, that joyous feeling of having it now comes over you. You feel happy, alive, and empowered. Desire is one of the most powerful feelings in the human experience. Never let someone talk you out of your desire. You have spent time and precious life energy bringing your desire this far. Think of how amazing you and everyone around you will feel as this idea becomes a reality.

Leave the "how it happens" to Divine Intelligence because it will put you on the journey and give you inspiration toward your desire. Have faith and believe. Act on inspired thought related to your desire. Summon any help you need by envisioning yourself already having it during your journey. Feel the essence of having this desire. Talk about it as one of the most important things in your life. Give it the power of your valuable, priceless thought. That is your job.

A good example of using these processes for me started back in 2009 when I began looking at condos at the time of the real estate crash. I was making a lot of trips to Florida and looking all up and down the sun (west) coast of Florida. I would walk in and see those views of the ocean, the floor to ceiling slider doors, the tile floor and all the amenities. It made me want a getaway of my own. The issue was that I had been laid off and given severance from the job I had, and since this was my main income (I have almost always had more than one), I was not in a position to get one of these on a "fire sale" like those going on during that time.

Fast forward a few years, and I had moved to the Washington, DC area and gotten a well-paying contract with a large telecom helping them roll out a new infrastructure so they would be compatible with the a new internet protocol. This took my income well back into six figures, and I was able to bank a fair amount of money. I had decided to start traveling abroad again since I had done so in the US Navy and enjoyed the time ashore in the foreign countries. I got my passport and looked for where I wanted to go. I searched around and saw that there were a lot of resort type condo developments in Thailand. I booked my ticket, rented a condo, and flew over there not even knowing what to expect. It is a LONG flight. This flight had me connecting several places in the USA and in Tokyo before finally landing in Bangkok. It was still another hour and a half car ride down to the beach area where I wanted to look for a condo.

I had looked on a Thai forum and read to be cautious about buying these properties from a plan unless the builder and real estate company were reputable. I found a Re/Max agent in the newer, modern mall next to the condo I was staying in, and she took me to the management office of a development company which was well-known for building these condo resorts. I was shown the land where they intended to build and a small model of what would be the completed property. I quickly developed a rapport with the sales manager and was sent home with a wealth of literature, pricing, and plans. A couple of days after I got home, I took a deep breath, went to the bank and wired a $10,000 deposit to the development company to start the journey to owning an 8th floor unit at the Amazon Residence near Jomtien Beach, in Thailand.

I made many more trips over there as the construction started and progressed. These trips got better and better as Emirates Airlines started flying out of my home airport near DC. I got to ride on the Emirates A380 on some of these trips. This is the Rolls Royce of aircraft. It's so smooth and quiet, and the second deck is dedicated to business and first class along with a lounge. It is part of the vacation when you fly on this airline.

After a few trips, and a construction delay because of immigration issues with the workers, I made a trip there three years to the month after I first looked at the land and property model. This trip was to GET THE KEY! I was so excited because I had paid on it over two years, and getting the key meant it was paid in full and was now mine. No payments other than utilities and yearly maintenance. A place of my own I can go to enjoy at any time. The lagoon pool is spectacular. The street vendor food in Thailand is second to none. I took a dream to fulfillment through making my want a desire and making a clear decision that this would indeed be mine. As of this writing, I visit this place two or three times a year and am able to rent it out when I am not there. It's an amazing feeling to get what I wanted mainly because I had conditioned my mind to accept this as possible and important to me.

Every person reading this book can follow many journeys like this in their lifetime. There are so many possibilities seeking expression RIGHT NOW that it is a given that fuller expression will be happening constantly throughout the existence of mankind. See it. Feel it. Invest your time and emotion into making it your desire. And then take that wonderful journey in faith to your heart's desire. You deserve it. You must absolutely make it happen. You will improve your life and the lives of everyone around you with every success.

TRUE AUTHENTICITY VERSUS CONFORMING

"The opposite of courage in our society isn't cowardice.
It is conforming."
~Rollo May

The most valuable gift you can give to yourself and those around you is to be your authentic self. Authenticity matters. Be yourself. Nobody can do it better than you. Be true to you. The best path to this way of being is to understand yourself as mentioned before in this book. Think about it this way: the easiest way to get your life where you want it to be is to talk about how you want things to be rather than how they are. Start talking about your life as best as it can be. You will soon be inspired with ideas on beginning that journey. No one has ever complained themselves into prosperity. Not one person. All dreams come true are the fulfillment of desires becoming reality. Be clear about the life you really want. This is true authenticity. This is courage in its truest form. This is you being the person you were created to be!

Also, allowing those around you to be authentic is important. Think of it this way: your journey is unique, and only you understand it the best. When you think someone is doing something "inappropriate," remember that is your perspective. The other's perspective is entirely different and sheds a different light on every subject in their life. Unless they have ASKED YOU to help them change, allow them to create their world as you create your own. All of these worlds are a blessing, and our intersection with them is a blessing as well. It is our job to find that blessing, not change the world of another.

Consider this as well: one of the things that causes people to get off track in life is worrying about others. Chances are you worry more about some of the people you care about more than they worry about themselves. This may even cause you to focus on their problems so much that they become your own. This is not a good situation to be in. Remember that worry is using your mind to create a situation that you *really DON'T* want. If you think about that situation you don't want long and hard enough, your life can perfectly resemble THAT worry. The best thing to do is this: trust them to do right by themselves. Trust yourself to do right by you. This will help your days improve as the worry about what might happen fades from your mind and its influence fades from your life.

Another perspective that holds people back is tied into the word "supposed." "It's what you are supposed to do or be." Look at the definition of supposed: "Generally assumed or believed to be the case, but not necessarily so." Doing what you believe you are "supposed to do" according to others' beliefs means you are allowing yourself to be controlled by other people, putting your own feelings for yourself second or at even a lower place. Ask yourself: Supposed by whom? Since when did this opinion become such a driving force in your life? Have you thought about if you really benefit from this "supposed" subject? Doing what you want to do, following your own desire, means you are in control of your life. You are A Unique Renegade. Unique Renegades are successful people because they think for themselves. They are free because they think for themselves. They are happy because… see where this is going? The Unique, Authentic Renegade is the happy, free, inspired person.

"Circumstances" are another area people blame for their problems. George Bernard Shaw talks about these "outer directed" people in this quote: "People are always blaming their circumstances for what they are. I don't believe in circumstances. The people who get on in this world are the people who get up and look for the circumstances they want, and if they can't find them, make them." So, if you don't see the circumstances you currently want, begin creating them. You absolutely DO NOT have to conform to circumstances you don't want. As we have said earlier, stop conforming, and look inside for the real truth. You and those around you will benefit if you believe in what you are creating. Using imagination mixed with a good dose of faith and passion, you can create circumstances that are VERY much to your liking. As people begin to appreciate your circumstances, they will begin to create their own which will help make your intersecting worlds very enjoyable to be a part of.

Allowing our sensory inputs to control us can take us off track, too. Through our senses of sight, smell, hearing, touch and taste, we can be bombarded, literally inundated, with useless, dramatic information if we allow it. Let's take yet another look at news. A relatively small amount of this "news" is useful. The rest is produced to get people emotionally involved, glued to the broadcast, and watching the commercials of the sponsors. It's so full of a certain political or dramatic perspective that it makes the person watching it wonder who is in control. The media carries a large part of the responsibility for influencing people's opinions by using this fear and drama to produce material that "sells." Material that sells is material that gets the higher ratings that advertisers pay for. The advertisers don't care about perspective; they just want buyers for their products. It doesn't matter if it is the mainstream media, "reality" TV, or talk radio. All of these mediums feed on fear and drama to get ratings. For example, the mainstream media emphasizes the attacks in the Middle East with up close, bloody footage. It tries to prove that the war is inevitable and plays on our fears of losing more of our troops. Talk radio wants you to feel the fear of terrorism every day. If you just tune in and listen for three hours a day, they will make sure you understand the nature of the enemy we are dealing with as if you didn't already. This collective fear has a powerful effect on the Law of Attraction that we really don't want. It is responsible to be informed, but no one needs to be flooded with huge amounts of endless information about what to fear or feel bad about in this moment.

Since the big "stories" get the big ads, consider cutting cable out of your life and making your OWN news. As mentioned before, get YOUR news from the Divine voice INSIDE. This is a far more inspiring way to live than allowing other people to tell you what is important. The truth is only you understand what is truly important to you. No broadcaster, drama queen, or any other person in your life can ever possibly understand what inspires you like you do. Take control of what is coming in. You'll be glad you did. Use a public internet medium like YouTube or Facebook Live to broadcast your beautiful, non-conformist life. It may be the next big movie. Who knows?

There are people in your life who will and want to influence your thinking if you allow them to. Of course, it's best not to. One good example is the "office grouch." This person always comes dashing in just in the nick of time, and you immediately find out how crummy their morning is a moment after this person arrives. "Traffic is horrible." "I couldn't get a decent parking space." "It took me an hour and 10 minutes to get here." "People don't know how to drive." "The coffee pot is empty." This is every day with this person. Through these thoughts, actions, and feelings, this person is invoking the Law of Attraction to guarantee a bad morning every day. It attracts more of the same daily. He or she should spend some time changing their "programming." This can be really bad when people let all of this "noise" affect them in the same way.

Another is the drama king or queen of the office. This can be quite a show. These people know the news and events of the day. They seem to be aware of everyone's tragedies. They know who divorced whom, whose kids are in trouble, who is having an affair. Interestingly enough, their lives seem to mirror all of these stories that fascinate them. Giving thought and feelings to these events is actually attracting them into their lives. So, of course, you hear their drama as well.

The person who talks most about disease has it. This is one of the worst things one can do for the health of the body. Clinical depression often results from dwelling on the outcome of a disease. When the human mind loses hope and dwells on how bad the disease is, the disease can get worse. There is a lot of scientific evidence about the mind playing a powerful role in healing the body. It's important that people see the difference between having high cholesterol and doing something about it and having high cholesterol and dwelling on how bad it is. Can you see who will have the stroke or heart attack? This and many other cases demonstrate that attitude is the difference in recovery or not.

So, the office grouch has approached you with his miserable morning, huh? A neat little trick for shifting a conversation from something you don't want to talk about to something you do is to simply tell the person, "That's interesting," and then change the topic. Say something complimentary about them, and the conversation will change immediately. People love to talk about themselves, so give them a great subject: something great about themselves. One enjoyable, inspiring conversation coming up!

Then we have the people who talk about the abundance they have. They are always glad for what they have. They also seem to bring a better standard of living into their lives with very little effort. They think in terms of prosperity. They see their lives as abundant. They have no problem getting the next position, attracting that new job, or even going out on their own to create prosperity. A lot of successful small business owners you meet will have a can do, positive attitude about everything in their lives. Challenges are a vehicle to learn from. They inspire creative thought in any situation. They are volunteers in their communities and often leaders at their churches or kids' sports teams. You never hear "I don't have time." Yet these are some of the busiest people you will meet.

There are the great teachers and philanthropists in our society. Many of these people went through hardships as bad as or even more difficult than what you have experienced or can imagine. They changed their reality by the single virtue of positive thought in all aspects of their lives. Instead of complaining, they found ways to be grateful. Instead of focusing on "I can't," they focused on "What can I do to..." and found a way. These people also have one thing in common. They always see the upside in any situation. They exude positive energy everywhere they go, and they attract positive people and events into their lives. The most important thing these people have learned is how to use their deepest gift to make the world a better place to live. They sincerely want people to live to the fullest of their ability. They enjoy lifestyles that most people only dream about. You will find them as authors, motivational speakers, business consultants and leaders of some of the most successful corporations on the planet. It is always a joy to hear these people speak. They get people to believe in themselves and often mentor those whom they see that "inspiring something" in. They make it their purpose to make the world a better place than they found it. They are as authentic as it gets. They are TRUE Renegades.

Your True Self: Who You REALLY Are

As we look at authenticity, it's important to look inside and discover who you really are. You will find that many people in your life, maybe even yourself, act out their life in such a way as to make all the people around them happy. They are "this person" to that person, and "another person" to someone else, and yet someone different to others. All of these "personalities" are a lot to keep up with especially if you don't even believe in "the person" you are acting like. This is why it's so important to show who you really are to the world and not try and be someone different to please someone else. They will never know who you really are or get the privilege of experiencing the "true self" that lives inside you. Showing the world your true self also attracts people with the same essence as you, so your sphere of friends will be MUCH more to your liking. Just think: What if that person you are "acting" for wants to develop a deeper relationship with the person you are playing instead of your true self? Better introduce yourselves NOW so the relationship can develop naturally. Give yourself the blessing of allowing everyone you come in contact with to discover who you really are. Now, things are much easier. Now, your sphere of influence likes you, and you really like it. Remember that being authentic requires self-understanding and being on a self-inspired journey. You will never meet an original copycat. Also, remember that in life there are Observers and Visionaries. The Observer is always confused by noise from the voices on the outside. The Visionary is always enlightened by louder, clearer voice on the inside. Keep yourself enlightened. As Richard Branson famously said, "Take a sledgehammer to conformity." Be the real you. Be as authentic as you can be. There is tremendous potential inside the true you that can change the world around you.

RELATIONSHIPS

The most important relationship anyone has is with themselves. A deep, authentic appreciation and personal self-esteem toward one's self is required. Don't confuse self-esteem and ego. There is an ultra-fine line between ego and self-esteem. Ego is purely about being above others and stems from the competitive mind. Self-esteem brings value to others through your appreciation of yourself. Self-esteem stems from the creative mind. Choose the way you perceive yourself with care. The right attitude about yourself benefits others and adds tremendous value to your journey. Being competitive assumes someone has to lose, and in a Universe with an unlimited supply of all that is good, that simply is not the case.

We enter relationships at many different points and for different reasons in our lives. When we take a job, join a group of people in support of something, travel to new places or find one we think could be our soul mate, a relationship is formed. It is important to understand this: once you have met someone, you are in an eternal relationship. You can't "unknow" somebody. All of life experience is like this. Every experience is part of the broader, more aware being you have become because of that experience. Something else to consider is that one of the most important things we are charged with as human beings is to find the best in others. Love and care for one another. See the good in yourself, and you will naturally see the good in others. This wonderful perspective will help us get the most out of the relationships we create.

In any relationship, agreements are far more effective than rules. "Welcome to my life. Now, here are the rules" is far more restrictive than

"Welcome to my life. Let's agree to make this partnership beneficial to both of us." Rules choke relationships. Agreements expand relationships. Telling someone what to do and how to do it holds them back. Agreeing with someone on what will be done and how expands both people, thereby improving the relationship. Agreements evolve from understanding what the other(s) want from the relationship and matching that up with what you want. It is necessary to find what you agree on and let the rest go unless it is something everyone agrees needs to be a part of the relationship. You then have to find a way to agree on the subject. Telling someone they are wrong will stop things a lot faster than saying, "Help me understand why this is important." Seeking mutual understanding will always open more doors than assuming another has to be wrong.

My own personal example of how I relate with others includes living with an open heart. In my mind, it's the only way to be truly authentic. Living with an open heart comes with a price...and I have paid it many times. I will gladly pay it again and again while showing people the best I can be. If they try to take advantage of me, that is on them, not me. I have to trust myself to bring the best people into my life and to allow those with different intentions to do as they will. If it doesn't feel right, I'll shift my focus from those who don't have my best interest in mind and seek out those who do. The power of choice is awesome. I apply this philosophy to all relationships I enter.

I also set some expectations for myself regarding the woman I want to bring into my life as I am single and open to possibilities as of this writing. It goes something like this:

She knows I am a man through and through. Anything less, she will test. And I want it that way.

My praise effortlessly opens her heart.

I relish her constantly changing moods. It means that she is woman through and through.

She expects me to make decisions and appreciates the decisions I make.

There is abundant joy in my heart because she chose me.

The Universe speaks through her to keep my life impeccably on track.

These are really expectations I have of myself in this relationship I am working on bringing into my life. Evoking this from that special someone will make her happy, and the end result of that is that I will be even happier.

I also wrote an affirmation which involves seeing this relationship as already mine. It goes like this:

I am so happy and grateful for my soul mate.

Like me, she is physically, emotionally, mentally and spiritually sexy.

She is radiant. She shines as love.

She makes me immensely glad to be a man.

How could I possibly miss this one when I see her? This is taking time, but I have all the patience I'll need to allow this to happen.

A Note on Harmony

Relationships thrive on harmony. This is such an important aspect of the life experience. Think about sound for a moment. Sound is a vibration. A radio speaker moves back and forth rapidly to produce the voices that you hear. How fast the speaker moves back and forth is expressed as the frequency of the vibration. Recall that thoughts from the mind are thought waves or frequencies. Frequencies that are in harmony with what you want will attract this into your life. You must "get in tune" with the life you want. Think of life in terms of songs. What are you in tune with right now? The music that moves you the most probably reflects how you view life. So, if you are always listening to sad, "relationship gone bad" songs and feeling the message in them, you will attract that type of relationship. Put on that tune that makes you dream of the best possible outcome. Imagine yourself in the place that song takes you. What are you going to attract? The good life you have always wanted. This applies to experiences, too. Many of the most enjoyable experiences in life are free or low cost. Do them to get yourself in tune with the best life has to offer. Go out and walk in nature. Find a group with the same interests you have, and visit with them often. Do what is in harmony with you inside, and you will find you are with people who enjoy what you do. Life will be a song you want repeated over and over. You will be amazed at the life you live if you are living "in tune" with the people you want to be associated with.

Be the type of human being you want in your life.

Groom yourself to attract what you want. The body comes across to others as much more attractive when you take care of it. This includes grooming. The image you want the world to have of you must be the image you present. Take care of your skin. Keep your hair the way you want people to see it. Maintain good dental hygiene. Make sure your smile shows the people around you what you want them to see. You are feeling good, so you will be smiling a lot, right? Most of the things you do to groom yourself are free or very inexpensive. These steps can make a very strong impression that you are as good as you feel. This is another step to attracting all that you want, including the people that will participate in making it happen. Taking care of yourself is taking care of your world. We all want the best from the world we are creating for ourselves. Always understand that YOU deserve the best. So, take care of yourself as though you deserve the best.

Exercise. Work it! Get the body and the energy you need to sustain yourself in your new, high performance life. It does not matter what condition you are in. Simply walking thirty minutes a day can do wonders for your health. As you become stronger, you can add exercise activities that fit your life and make you feel much better. Do your exercise in a place that brings joy to your heart. When you exercise, stay in your comfort zone. You have better, more lasting results exercising this way. Do not exhaust your body because your muscles work better when oxygen is plentiful in the blood. If you are short of breath, oxygen is in short supply! You will benefit more by doing exercise that is within your capability, based on your own current conditioning. Your endurance will increase faster. You will run less risk of exercise related injury. The goal of your exercise is feeling good through increased stamina and energy. Unless you are a competing athlete, do not concern yourself with what other people do for exercise. Create the best plan for yourself. Competition with others has nothing to do with your own conditioning. Do what leaves you feeling invigorated, alive, and refreshed. Be creative. Mix it up. Create a plan that challenges your body and leaves you fresh and recharged afterwards. The better you feel, the more you will feel a desire to make exercise a required part of your daily routine. Your increased energy will exude wellbeing to all of those around you. You will likely find people wanting to join you in your quest for fitness. This will be yet another enjoyable, simple process that helps create the life and relationships you want.

Love your body because it is a miracle in and of itself. Think of how you were created. Your parents, thought, love, and the energy of the Universe created it. Every person on this earth is an amazing creation. Your body is always in and part of the creative process. It is constantly healing and renewing itself. Think of how your body was designed to be. See your body as the true manifestation of the Creative Source and the Universe that it really is. You have your own body temple to be proud of. It is the Divine home of your Spirit. Appreciate it just as you appreciate the home you live in. This self-esteem is stronger than anything someone can or will ever say about you. You are the Master of Your Own Life. Your opinion of your body is far more important than anyone else's. Your love for your body will cause you to make it the best it can be. And as you appreciate it, others will, too. Notice how the people around you with the best self-esteem also tend to be the most loved by themselves and others.

Enjoy your body. It was made to get the best out of this physical environment you are in. You have senses which give you the ability to enjoy life to its fullest. Use your sight to enjoy the variety of life in all of its colors, shapes, and sizes. Hear the magic of life as it roars past in the form of a roar of thunder chasing the wind or as absolute silence on a quiet afternoon. Smell, taste, and enjoy the meal created for you. Feel the temperature and texture all around you. Enjoy the touch of the person most intimate with you in that very moment. In this living Universe, life is constantly being created for you to enjoy with your body. This is the creative process showing you how your life is at this very moment. Your body was made with all you need to experience – everything that life on earth has to offer. You can use your creative mind to put yourself in a position to see, hear, smell, taste and feel more of what you want in life. Become a match to it, and more will manifest in your life.

As you can see, your body is a masterpiece that is the home for your Spirit while you are alive here on earth. If you can't be happy with yourself, you certainly won't be happy with anyone else. Find your own joy! Being the best you can be will tend to attract the type of people you want to enter a relationship with. Everyone wants the best for themselves, and the best way to that end is to be the best you can be. Remember also that "moral compass" is individual. You were born with values unique to you, and as you move into alignment with those, you feel very good. When you move out of alignment with those, you don't feel as good. Remember that everyone else's morals are unique to them as well. The morals of another do not necessarily apply to you. People tend to believe that there is only one set of morals for everyone. Part of what makes humans unique is having their OWN values and morals. It is through the misconception of "absolute values" or "only one set of morals to live by" that every law and religious belief starts as one begins trying to protect another or others from others. You will find that the most inspiring people around do not live in fear of anything they feel they need to be protected from. They live from faith through understanding. They always seem to find themselves in a very safe, happy environment. This is because they understand that worry and joy can't occupy the same space in the mind. They choose joy, and the things people want protection from simply don't show up in their lives. This means that when we live true to ourselves, we don't need this kind of protection.

You will become what you think about just as the people around you will become what they think about. Think about a life with ALL of the right people in it. They will show up to the party as soon as you do. That will make this a party that all involved will want to be a part of. Take care of yourself, and become THAT person because you are worth it. Another good reason is because it will inspire you to take care of your relationships making your life that much more grand. Make all of the relationships you form worthy of you. How you feel about yourself is a strong indicator of how you feel about others.

HEALTH

In our journey toward the health we desire, it is only necessary to hyphenate the word healthy to see what thought process we should employ to get where we want to be. When we hyphenate the word healthy, it is heal-thy. You can apply this to whatever you want to be healthy. Think "heal-thy Spirit, heal-thy body, etc." Using this type of affirmation is a good way to ask for the healing you want. When you ask, you will be inspired to the right action for this moment. Remember that asking for good health is imagining the health you want as if you already have it. See yourself as a perfectly human being enjoying all that life has to offer. It is always the best thing to make great health one of your top desires. Let the doctor take care of the treatment for the physical symptoms, and you take care of keeping that vision and desire for a strong, healthy body and Spirit in the front of your mind.

Our health is the result of a very complex relationship between our conscious and subconscious selves and our physical body. As we hyphenated heal-thy, we can hyphenate dis-ease. Dis-ease is a description of a body that is not at ease. There is an enormous supply of literature and help on this subject. Much of modern medicine is based around the treatment of symptoms of a dis-ease rather than the healing of the human being as a whole. The relationship between large pharmaceutical companies and health care organizations focuses more on the treatment of the symptoms of the ailment being "treated" than the true cure. Always research those who have found the cure versus those who succumb to dis-ease. Focus on dis-ease will only create more dis-ease. Proof of this is that you rarely see a healthy person talk about the dis-ease that is present in his or her body.

Our Two Vital Energies

The human being, as we know it, has two distinct energies: the body and the Spirit. Just as your home is the place you live, your body is the home your Spirit lives in. Mind is the motion of the Spirit, and the body is the living reflection of that motion. If you have a desire, large or small, the physical part of bringing that desire to you is done by your Spirit moving the body through thought. An example is being thirsty. Your Spirit recognizes the body's need for liquid and helps form thoughts that cause you to walk to the refrigerator and get what you want to drink. That is an example of conscious thought. Conscious thought is thought which is caused by the want to do or experience something. We can form the thought from nothing, which is the source of our imagination. We can also form thoughts based on what we observe, hear, or feel. These thoughts are a response to what is in this moment of our lives. Our conscious thoughts, when repeated enough, impress images on our subconscious and manifest themselves in reality if we become emotionally invested in them.

Spiritual Health

Nourishing our Spirit is important. What you feed the subconscious is the most influential thing there is when it comes to being the Unique Renegade you want to be. Remember that the subconscious mind is like fertile soil. What you plant there will grow. As the reflection of a living Spirit, your body's senses along with your emotions tell you very clearly if you are feeding your subconscious the right things. This is essential to living the best life possible. For most people, this means a significant shift in what and how they think. If you spend most of your time focusing on what you do not want, you must stop now because as you focus on it, you make its presence in your physical life stronger. Without neglecting your responsibilities, shift the focus of your thoughts, imagination, and desire to what you want in life. Begin to impress clear images in your subconscious to give your Creator the thoughts on the life you want. He is always listening and responding. Make this an exercise you repeat over and over until the idea or image is second nature to you. Get emotionally involved with the image to move it from an idea to a desire. You will then act on instinct from what was once just an idea. You will recall it easier and the thoughts will inspire the actions that will bring it into your life that much quicker.

At this time you may be thinking or even worried about all of the negative thoughts you have impressed on your subconscious. Please don't worry about this for another instant. It is proven scientifically that a positive thought is hundreds of times more powerful than a negative thought. What does this mean to you? It means no matter where you are, you can put things into your subconscious that are positive and start to feel good right away. There are habits you have formed that are not in line with what you really want out of life or who you REALLY are. Look at all of your habits including thought patterns that occur daily as a reaction to daily life. Work to replace the ones that make you feel bad with ones that make you feel good. This is an important step to being the Unique Renegade you want to become since the positive will overwhelm the negative in your subconscious. Anything that makes you feel good will place these images on the subconscious and send them to Divine Intelligence. You will see problems begin to dissolve, and life will feel really good. Give yourself the best gift you can: the ability to be the star player in your own life through inspired thinking.

Physical Health

When our bodies don't feel their best, it is difficult to focus on what we want to accomplish. There are countless dis-eases out there. Notice again that the word dis-ease has been hyphenated here. Remember that simply means a body that is not at ease. The first and most essential part of true healing is to get your mind on what good health feels like to the best of your ability. Allow the doctor to specify the medication that will help the body heal from the disease. Your responsibility simply lies in focusing on the desire to feel better.

This is especially true with a very unwanted diagnosis. I have a story which demonstrates the *will* to heal when I was being told there was little hope for improvement. I had been diagnosed with congestive heart failure. This happens when the amount of blood pumped through the lower left chamber of the heart is too low. It is expressed as ejection fraction, meaning the fraction of the blood ejected when the heart squeezes. Normal runs from 50% at the low end to 70+ % at the high end. Mine was only 19%! I was tested again two months later and told no change. The doctors at this practice also did not give me a decent chance of rehab, and they specified treatments that made no sense to me. Consequently, I fired them and started working with another doctor. He was more optimistic about my exercise regimen and goal of recovery. We scheduled another test to check the heart's capacity out, and I had gone to 50%! This happened in a matter of a little over four months. I was looking at the recovery rate after cardio exercise, and as it was improving, I was feeling better. As it turns out, the best prescription was will and a cardio rehab program I set up and believed in. I am now in the process of working with the doctor to ween myself from the medications I'm taking to control the heart. I was healed primarily by the cardio routine I employed and continue to follow.

What can we glean from this? We must understand that within every problem, there is a solution. For every dis-ease, there is a body AT ease. As we have said before, when you get the news of your body not being at ease, immediately start your research to find those who *found their way back to wellbeing* from a spot like or similar to what you have just discovered. The routine that I followed has been used by a close friend of mine to recover from his own diagnosis of heart failure. He has since made the seven day foot trek to Mount Everest base camp in Nepal. The key point here is that no one ever gets completely healthy by focusing on dis-ease. We have to align our Spirit with the wellbeing we desire for our body to begin to heal and go in that direction. This means that during the healing process, one must keep his or her mind on what it is like to feel 100% healthy. Remember heal-thy. Come up with affirmations which offer gratitude for the healing that is going on inside at the present moment. The body is made up of cells, and every cell is always seeking wellbeing. Every cell is connected to the mind. Feed your cells the wellbeing they want by doing anything that will result in your feeling happier and better in the moment. What goes on in our minds has an amazing effect on the wellbeing of the bodies we live in. Giving praise for all things that heal-thy while one is healing will help a person heal-thy self faster. It is important enough to repeat: find the stories of those who came back from the dis-ease you may be facing. Do as much as you can like what they did to heal.

Health is an area of your wellbeing where harmony is an absolute requirement. You have to be in harmony with what you want to feel like. The results we call health are the outcome of the thoughts we think and our bodies' response to those thoughts. If you are thinking and emotionally invested in what you do not want, your body can and sometimes will develop dis-ease as a result of the emotions of worry or stress. In fact, worry often sets up stress which makes the body much more vulnerable to dis-ease. The dis-ease is often a message to us: we are not loving or joyful in a certain area of life. Research and find out what bodily symptoms are related to the dis-ease you are experiencing while allowing the doctor to treat the symptoms of the dis-ease. As you find answers, you can start to change things one at a time until you see the health improvement you are looking for. Keep your mind tuned into what makes you feel good.

When you see and feel the improvement, stay on that road since it has been shown to help your body become healthier. Persistence is very important here. Stay on course, and use your will to bring yourself into alignment with what you want.

SUCCESS, MONEY, AND BUSINESS

All businesses have a purpose and a goal. The purpose is related to the product or service being offered. The goal is always to make a profit. A growing business is one that is profiting, and a dying business is one that is losing money. Most businesses tie their purpose to a vision. When the vision of a business is clear, attracting the right employees is much easier. Clients get much better service because the employee believes inside that he or she is part of something that is a reflection of how they feel. People respond very well when they are informed of the direction the place they work is going. Financial goals are reached more often because everyone knows what it will take to get from where the business is in this moment to the goals management has envisioned. Since they feel positive and safe, employees have much less fear of saying something when there is a problem that needs to be addressed. All of this creates what is seen as a responsive, nimble business in the marketplace. Business illustrates the powerful effect of a strong, clear vision, and the ability to have the laws working in each person to make the business thrive. Just remember that ideas create wealth. It is never the other way around. Think about it.

In the same way good energy sends a business forward, not so good things can happen when just one person in the management team is concerned more with his or her status in the organization than the vision of the business. People who report to this person are always under stress because they are being micromanaged. Everything is an emergency. There is a "revolving door" of employees coming and going because the atmosphere is not conducive to employee development or the overall vision of the business. People work long hours and feel very bad when they leave to go home. Through the Divine Law, all of these people attract things into their lives that make them even less productive as employees. The domino effect should be obvious in this case. When every person in the department talks about how bad it is, then every person in the department feels how bad it is, then the result is how bad it is. A shift in awareness by the person running the team can have a huge impact on the success of the department and the business as a whole.

Respect is never a given; it is earned. See yourself receiving respect, and part of that vision must be having it as well. You give, then ask through the vision of respect, get in the feeling place of what you want and then receive it. If you have self-respect, if you feel respect for yourself inside, you will offer it to others like yourself. Others will offer respect to you. Guess what? Again, like attracts like. Respect attracts respect. It does not matter if you are a manager or report to one. Respect can never be demanded. Those who demand respect rarely ever have respect for themselves. Self-respect will earn the respect of others every time. A lack of self-respect along with demanding respect from others will lose respect every time. Respect yourself. Respect from others will be the result.

One thing businesses sometimes do is compete their way out of business. It is important to understand that in the business world, the successful business engages their creative side and has no need to compete. You have seen this type of business before. Any of their sales staff operates on a level so much higher, it closes out the competitive part of the mind and fully engages the creative side. When competition is in play, it assumes a loser. True professionals create and, therefore, leave themselves in position to win at all times. Remember that, as Personal Performance Mentor Bob Proctor has said, "Amateurs Compete. Professionals Create." Engage in business at a highly creative level, and you won't have any meaningful competition.

If you are in a leadership position in a business, and you want to continue moving up, you must understand and always be creating the vision of the company. People who believe in the company, and are positive about this belief, will bring all of the positive aspects of Divine Laws with them. If you are one of these people, it will be evident to all of those around you that you are someone who can be counted on to get the job done. The people who report to you will feel this, and it will have a positive impact on their attitude toward their responsibility. If you are in a position that you don't like, plan on being there for a while or even not retaining that position. The best thing to do in this situation is to find a job that you feel good about, and seek work in that field. Become educated if you have to. Remember that the Law of Attraction states that like attracts like. That means that it stands to reason if you don't like your work, it doesn't "like" you much either. Get into an environment where you can tune in to what is going on, and watch your success grow.

In management, good leadership is essential. Think about what Chris Haggerty wrote: "The goal of most leaders is to get people to think highly of them as a leader, but the goal of the exceptional leader is to get people to think highly of themselves." Be the creative, exceptional leader. Make certain that your team is empowered to do everything they are capable of to help the business succeed. Help make the personal connections necessary for your team to thrive. When a business succeeds, the bottom line gets better, and personal compensation is not too far behind. Make sure your team thinks as highly of themselves as possible. A team that feels good about itself is a powerful team. They experience success and represent the company well.

If you report to a manager, be an intelligent follower. Like the leaders, always be creating the vision of your business just as your leadership must. While you are at work, your responsibility is to be a resource the business can use to grow. If you know the vision of the company and feel good about it, projects assigned to you will be done well because they are coming from your belief in the business. Understand the management at all levels. Make sure you know who is in charge of what part of the business. Create and build the relationships around the company that you will need to succeed in your projects. Many times you will need resources from other parts of the business to accomplish your task. Instead of coming to your manager with, "It can't be done," identify your problem to him or her, and ask "What can I do to get this done?" You will always receive a better response because you are seen as a doer and not a quitter. You will find the path to the end result most of the time and learn along the way. This attitude gets people promoted to better positions. Work smarter instead of harder. Get noticed. And begin to attract the life you want.

Whether in a leadership or reporting role, if you are working for an organization that operates on a competitive philosophy, keep your mind on the creative plane while you are working there. Be open to new opportunities with creative businesses. As you keep your mind in the creative mode, you will become a match to creative business, or you may influence your department to operate as a creative unit and demonstrate that the ideas of your team have more success potential than those the organization has been using to compete and "take other business." Remember that profit realized from the competitive mindset is easily here today and gone tomorrow. The business that operates on a highly creative level produces goods and services that its customers always come back for more of. Goals from creative ideas are more consistently attained because of the enthusiasm that is behind creative ideas.

Good goal setting skills are one of the most important things a person can have. These skills keep your mind focused on what you have decided on accomplishing. As Robert A. Heinlein wrote, "In the absence of clearly-defined goals, we become strangely loyal to performing daily trivia until ultimately we become enslaved by it." Let's take a closer look at what "daily trivia" is and what it does to set us back in accomplishing our desires. Often, one's day goes something like this. They wake up and the thoughts from yesterday's trivia are the first thing that come to mind as they are the most recent moment this person consciously lived. We can pause to define this trivia. It's a routine. It's the programming we talked about earlier in the book that drives this routine. Since this person has no real, powerful desire driving them, they only pay attention to what their *routine* presents to them as their current reality. To change current reality, the subconscious needs something BIGGER than the daily trivia one is living. This person needs to set a clearly-defined goal that is, once again, BIGGER than the trivia he or she is living. This involves getting in tune with the feeling he or she will have *when their daily routine matches what they really WANT to feel in life*. No subject is off the table. Everything from the job to the money to the home to the leisure activity.....EVERYTHING is fair game. This life is a one-time play, and YOU are the star. Does it feel like you are the star of something special? If not, engage those marvelous mental faculties you have, and GET TO WORK. Set your goal!

There are several steps to coming up with a goal. When an idea is inspired, and you want to explore it further, the first step is to reason with it and start getting excited about it. Hold it on the screen of your mind. Begin to visualize what your life will look like with this idea as a reality. Continue to come up with reasons for bringing this idea to life. At the right time, you will have impressed it on your subconscious mind and can make a decision to move forward with it. As soon as you have made this decision, it is now a goal. Many of the smaller, supporting things around the idea will start to appear in your life because of the decision you made. Keep this goal alive by writing the end result down on a card small enough to carry in your pocket. Be specific. If it is a monetary goal, state exactly how much the income or amount will be. Also, state what you are willing to give in return for the money. Read it regularly. As you read it, the goal will be more and more a part of your default way of thinking. You will then find your way to the goal very quickly. Once you achieve this goal, it's time to come up with a larger, even more fulfilling, goal. Like last time, write it down. Keep using your amazing mind to bring it to life. Always remember how anything important to mankind came into being – as a single thought in someone's mind.

A few notes about the size of your goals. Get OUT OF your comfort zone. There is little fulfillment in setting a goal that you are already familiar with how to accomplish. Show some guts and faith, and declare that true desire deep inside your heart. It should excite you. It should take you where you have never been before developmentally. "How" does not matter as much as "what" with faith behind it. Edison did not know how the first incandescent light bulb would work; he just knew that through faith and increased understanding that it would. Many ideas are conceived with no idea of how. How is Divine and always shows up at just the right time through faith. Make your goals as big and beautiful as your imagination will let you. You have so much to offer the world. Also consider that all inventions, circumstances, and experiences come from ideas which come from thought. Every thought offered is eternal and, therefore, shapes eternity. As we create on earth, we create in eternity as well. Do you like your contribution to eternity? If not, is now not a good time to improve the ideas you are offering?

Selling by Heart

One thing that is absolutely certain is that if a business is not reaching the hearts of its clients, it won't be selling as much as it could. Throughout this book, we have spoken about the creative versus the competitive mindset, and there has never been a doubt in my mind that the creative sales person is the one I will want to do business with. I will strive to be that sales person when I am selling as well. If you are in a sales position, your job is to create desire in your prospective client's heart just as you do for yourself when you really want something. Think about it this way: you have a person with an idea, a small vision of what they want right in front of you. This is the best opportunity in the world to co-create with that person and move that idea from the conscious mind to the emotional mind which IS the subconscious mind. I think you can tell that the creative mindset has a huge advantage here in that you are striving to work with the part of your client's mind that runs their life daily. It does not matter what you are selling. The point is to get that emotional investment going.

Let's look at the difference between processes of competitive and creative selling. As seen at several points in this book, competitive selling assumes a loser. If the salesman sees himself as a winner in the successful transaction, who is the loser? If "Got him!" runs through the salesman's mind, what does that say about the clients standing in the salesman's mind? Think about how some car salesmen will guilt their client into paying more or buying the model they don't want. That client ends up "overpowered" by the salesman and, in a competitive atmosphere, is the loser. When the client is part of a "quota," or just a number to the sales person, there has to be a loser. The client is the loser if he buys, and the salesman is the loser if the client leaves and does not buy. This salesman competes with clients. He competes with his fellow salesmen. He is driven only by money. Relationships do not matter.

Now, let's look at the creative salesman. This is the salesman we need more of in the world. He takes a moment of genuine interest to find out what brought the client here to start with. He starts by beginning a relationship, not with "if we can get our numbers to match,… blah, blah, blah, blah." This person looks for leads in unusual places and engages them in a non-pressured way. "I saw you were looking at SUVs on the Smallville Lexus website. Are you looking for something for a family?" Boom. Instant magnetism. The interest in one's family will always bring down barriers and help form a positive, new relationship. Now, we are on our way to a far more pleasant transaction. Then, on to more relationship building questions and getting into what the customer's desire is. As soon as our salesman finds this out, it's time to get more specific. "Here is the SUV you want and its final price with all incentives. We just got the estimate for your trade, so it looks like your final cost will be <the total cost of the discussed vehicle>." Look at how this transaction centered around the desire and family of the client. The product being sold was a result of the relationship built by the salesman from the client's visit to the dealer website. Nice, creative way to move that transaction to a close.

I had a recent transaction work out this way. I had a vehicle I wanted to trade after an unexpected warranty repair raised a red flag for me. The check engine light came on with only 15,000 miles on the car, and an emissions part failed that I was not comfortable with. I got it back from the warranty repair and put out a request for trade in value to several dealerships. One came in 3-6000 dollars higher than the others, so I searched the inventory and found the car I liked. This one had an engine that came in about one out of a hundred of this model, and it had all the features I wanted: black exterior, tan leather interior, sunroof, all of the luxury features I wanted. A salesman emailed me back and asked if I'd like to drive the car. I didn't reply back immediately, expecting the standard salesman process, and he emailed back a few hours later saying, "Okay, let's do this your way. What's the next step? Do you want to drive a car, or do you have questions?" I liked this response much better and responded back asking about the offer they had made on my other car, and he said, "Bring it in, and as long as it is as described, that is what we will pay for the car." He also sent me a very competitive price on the car I wanted with all incentives included. This voice inside me was saying, "too easy." I cleaned out my trade and went to the dealer. The salesman got the key from me and let me drive the car I picked from the internet. I liked the car, so I asked him about the trade, and he simply said, "We're good." It was night, so I took my old car home, and we wrapped up the deal the next day with financing at a lower rate than my previous loan. Cherry on top. As you can see, this was literally a NO HAGGLE DEAL. The salesman was interested in getting me into the car that would make me the happiest, and he had to pull no tricks to do it. This made me a happy camper. (I have not mentioned brands to avoid any legal issues with the maker of the car I traded.)

This all goes to show that the salesman who takes time to understand his clients and their needs, and gets creative with the product or service offered, will close more deals than the guy to tries to wedge the deal in at the expense of someone else. The truth is that in the business world, there is absolutely NO need for competition or a loser when every bit of the Universe is all about expansion and fuller expression.

Personal Finance and Debt

Let's take a look at the personal relationship one has with money. In its most basic form (before the paper notes we see and associate with it), money is currency which is the energy of value transferred from one person or entity to another. This value has units in all national economies. In the USA and Canada, the unit is dollars unique to the country. In most of Europe, it is the Euro. In Thailand, it is the Thai Baht. There are many others. The value of these currencies compared to each other is called the *exchange rate*. The point here is that these different units of currency are transferred to a person or organization for goods or services. The amount given for goods and services is expressed as the *cost* of that which is being obtained in exchange for the money. Most everything you use or consume in life has a cost associated with it. All that you eat, wear, the place you live, the energy you use, all has a cost. Understanding this, we can say that life as a whole has a cost associated with it, and the lifestyle you live is going to be based on how much money is coming into your life. In all countries, money is always being printed. Like everything else in the Universe, there is an ever increasing supply of money, and money comes to people in various different ways including jobs and direct payment for services or goods. How much money is coming into your life determines how much you can buy to a large extent. To pay for something, you can use money directly or obtain credit, which is a promise that you will pay the person or entity for their service or product later. This credit is otherwise referred to as debt once the money has been loaned. At this point, the money is paid back in installments with interest added. Interest is an amount of money banks charge for lending money. People and businesses use credit to buy things with a higher value than they currently have in money. A home or car is a good example of things that cost more than most people have in money. So, they get a loan from the bank to pay for these "big ticket" items, and they pay the bank back on a monthly basis. This debt can be a tremendous help to people in the form of getting things they may not be able to afford otherwise. It can also end up crippling someone if they borrow too much and put themselves in a position where they can't make all of their payments every month. Make sure you don't obtain too much for the amount of money you have coming in. Ensure that you are able to afford all of the expenses that come along in your life. If money is short, look at options to bring more in as illustrated in the section below.

Create Your OWN Economy

Most people derive their income from selling time and skills to the place they work in exchange for a paycheck. The issue with this is that if the company delivering the paycheck does not need you anymore for whatever reason, your income is gone. Businesses, wealthy people, cities, towns and nations have one thing in common. They are economies, not employees. They derive income from much more than one single source. If they lose one, they can still thrive.

What is an economy? And why is it important to understand this? Per Wikipedia, "economy is defined as a social domain that emphasizes the practices, discourses, and material expressions associated with the production, use, and management of resources. Economic agents can be individuals, businesses, organizations, or governments." In other words, an economy is affected by everything flowing to and through it. The purpose of any economy, business or public, is to best channel the resources of the economy for the use of the beneficiaries of that economy. For business, this means customers, employees, and stock holders. In market based economies, the benefits of these resources are directed at the population who are the users of what the economy produces. Now, I want you to pay very close attention to the last sentence of the Wikipedia description of economy. "Economic agents can be individuals..." and stop right there. YOU can be an economy. The wealthiest people on earth are indeed large economies by themselves. They have businesses and employees the world over. You can, too. You should, too. This happens when an idea is so successful that it begins to outgrow its creator's capacity to serve all of its needs. At this point, the creator must add to the economy by hiring qualified help, outsourcing some of the work and, in many cases, securing mentorship to make sure the idea keeps growing as he or she now envisions. The most successful creators on earth are living, breathing economies making the lives of thousands, even millions, better by the thought of a single idea.

Let's look at the basics of what creates an economy. We have the products and services. We have the demand for those products and services. We have the producers of those products and services. And we have the cost for those products and services along with the profit from those products and services. The profit is figured from the full cost of the products and services including production, marketing, shipping and advertising subtracted from the cost of the products and services. No business or economy will thrive without a profit.

From our understanding of an economy, we can see that a person can become very successful, wealthy, and happy by having his or her own economy. This economy will not be predicated on the income of just one job. It will be supplied by many sources of income. The security this provides can't be underestimated. The gap between what you understand and what you offer the world out of that understanding is very likely tremendous. Every subject you understand well has intellectual value tied to it. It can be marketed and sold to those who want the service or product YOU can offer. I am not saying to make any sudden change right now, but you CAN make a decision to share all of your gifts with the world. This may involve getting or hiring help of some sort, refining your skills, but you can be the center of an economy with a large number of incomes. Then, you can become one of the happiest unemployed people in the world because you don't work for a company – you OWN it!

The ideas that will inspire you the most will come from inside or the Divine. It's easy to read something and become inspired, but it is far more rewarding to think of something that leaves you inspired. True inspiration that can change your life always comes from within. We grow the most when we fulfill the desires that we have set for ourselves. The path to those desires creates the growth from the problem solving we do while seeking the end result. Keep your eye on the ball, and the problem solving does get easier. It becomes difficult when we let the small things distract us. Desire + Focus + Determination = Success. It's a matter of wanting it enough and staying the course.

Masterminding

In *Think and Grow Rich*, Napoleon Hill wrote about the Mastermind Group principle as: "The coordination of knowledge and effort of two or more people, who work toward a definite purpose, in the spirit of harmony." In a business environment, you have many people in a common place with each person creating their own reality. So, let's look at how to make all of these people more successful for themselves and the company. This is a cumulative effect of many people being in tune with each other. It allows getting more things done by combining the creative power of many people. It can give one idea the power of the will and imagination of multiple minds. As all of the people in a Mastermind Group get emotionally invested in the idea, the power they are focusing on this idea takes a quantum leap. It is how drawings become tall buildings. It is how seemingly impossible dreams come to life. The power of many people with their thoughts in harmony should never be underestimated. For it is the power of the human mind multiplied that can turn a single thought into reality. If you appreciate the power of mastering your own reality, imagine the power when a group of people in harmony master the reality of one common vision. If all of the people feel good about what they are doing and have the same understanding of the goal, the resulting harmony will attract the success to the project felt by each person.

How to create a Mastermind? Get a group of likeminded people together, and meet when any member of the group has any kind of issue they want addressed and at scheduled times. The size is dependent on the focus of the group. Several important things to remember about a Mastermind Group. The members are there for what they can contribute. It's all about giving.

Members also have to understand how to graciously receive in order to gain the most value they can. That means gratitude and surrendering your mind to the group that has assembled to help you. When someone else calls a meeting, do your best to make the meeting, and contribute whatever you can to this person's request. This helps everyone in the group because all will benefit from the new ideas that emerge from the group.

It's a great idea to have Masterminds Groups in your private and business life. We want the best for ourselves which means, by necessity, we want the best for others. Create a Mastermind in your life, and give what you can for others. Be grateful and graciously receive as well. Make sure that you contribute to the harmony of the Mastermind Group. You will be amazed at the quantum leap that contributing to this brings to your life. This is another miracle that is the result of working in harmony with a living Universe.

SOCIETY'S BELIEFS AND THEIR OUTCOMES

You will notice that true freedom is rare in our society. Most people live a restricted life based on what they are paying attention to in the current moment. Attention invokes the Law of Attraction every time because of the feelings it creates. People have an immediate reaction to news stories and current events. You hear a huge number of "I don't want" or "This is what's wrong with" statements. What most of these people don't realize is that you can't say no about it or harbor angry or resentful feelings about it because the Law of Attraction brings more of what you push against. Look at these examples of the movements we have in society and the possibilities for a better result:

Mothers against Drunk Drivers: Drunk driving continues with more, not less arrests. This should be the Mothers' Movement for Designated Drivers with the emphasis on what we can do to correct the problem versus emphasizing the pain of losing a loved one.

War on Drugs: Has definitely brought more drugs and dangerous new ones since it started. We should take the billions we spend on this and turn it into a movement for the rehabilitation of drug addicts. Invest some into equipping law enforcement to detect driving under the influence of any mind-altering substance. Most can only screen for alcohol.

Anti-war Rallies: The radicals who hold and support these rallies always make the war supporters look more intelligent through their excessively emotional behavior. Marching at the funeral of a deceased son or daughter is hardly a way to persuade people to abandon a war. It will always strengthen the support of that war. March in support of peace with true empathy felt for the families' loss of a fellow human being. As Mother Teresa once said, "I was once asked why I don't participate in anti-war demonstrations. I said that I will never do that, but as soon as you have a pro-peace rally, I'll be there." Very wise words indeed. Don't protest against what you DON'T want. Rally for what you DO want.

The U.S. War on Illegal Immigration: One look at this one, and you cannot come to any other conclusion. The negative tone carried with this makes it a political lightning rod that neither major party wants to address. The result has been an open door all along the Mexican border with the potential for terrorists to enter this country unchecked. The U.S. has millions of illegal immigrants with no way to account for them. The taxpayer ends up supporting them through Medicaid and, sometimes, welfare. The most effective way to address this is a massive legal immigration movement. Make it possible for employers and people who want to immigrate to get together as easily as possible at the border or through easily obtained work visas. Secure the physical border as every other industrialized nation has.

The Fight Between the Two Major Parties

This is one of the issues that really engages the competitive side of the mind and stymies the creative side. The entire political system in the U.S. is mostly filled with hyper competitive lawyers who have a strong "can't be wrong" attitude. The people we elect to serve us end up being some of the least creative people on the planet because they spend their time "fighting" (read competing) for what is "right" with no consideration for creating real solutions for real problems in our world. Simply ask yourself: What was the last really creative thing you saw come out of an elected official? It sure would be inspiring for some of these people to imagine an idea that produces positive change in the world. Another thing to consider is that we should always be scrutinizing the goals of those who run to wield power over us, as most politicians do. When any person feels the need to have power over another, the problem lies with that person, not the one he wants power over. Every time. Be aware of your candidates' stated vision in relationship to their public record. More times than not, they don't align.

Instead of joining groups that spend their entire livelihood looking for what's wrong, find people who are in tune with your beliefs, and read their work. Seek out the good news. There is a lot of it, but the mainstream media considers it the "lighter side of the news," so you won't find much there. Get into the internet, the library, and small local newspapers to find the things to feel good about. Get involved with activities that make you feel good, and make your own news. Write about it. Start a newsletter about everything good in your department at work, and send it companywide. Your enthusiasm will begin to affect the feelings of people around you.

If you are in any kind of group or organization that protests strongly against things that it doesn't believe in rather than having a positive message geared toward helping the community, consider finding another organization that is in harmony with what you know and feel is right. Protesting is a competitive mindset. Protesters are not operating from a creative perspective. Some churches oppose something so strongly, they do not realize they are merely making it stronger by collectively stating and feeling what they do not want. They must find a positive, creative way to impact their community and achieve their mission.

Any culture, whether it is a business, city, group or otherwise, has a collective ability to change things around it through combined focus. Be aware of what people around you are doing and saying so that you don't get caught up in any issues you don't believe in or feel discord with. Do your best to put yourself where the common goal is one you share with others.

When it comes to news and information, find out only what you need to know, and then go about guiding your own thoughts so that you stay safe and positive. Don't let public information control you. Be your own informant. Your own internal voice must be louder than the voices outside to be the Unique Renegade you want to be.

DECIDE AND THEN ACT!

Decision is the polar opposite to procrastination. What you will find is that the most successful people are the ones who make decisions quickly. They are also very slow to change their minds if they do at all. The power behind this is persistence. Keeping your mind on what you want to feel like is an excellent method of getting what you want. This is because the reason behind wanting ANYTHING is that we believe we will feel better by having it. Everyone deserves to feel fantastic.

This is an area of people's lives where they almost never complete the actions that will change their subconscious mind. So many people say out loud, "God will take care of it." Then they stop giving the subject any thought and become sad or angry when the outcome they had in mind for "God to take care of" did not happen. The other problem that can occur is that they will pray in words at a certain time every week. They will "worship God" by spending time with a group of people so focused on what is wrong with the world, they will collectively create more of it. This is EXACTLY why, in many cases, what they did not want happened. When we look at this honestly, it's a really lazy way of thinking and should leave anyone with higher faculties, like all human beings have, disappointed in themselves. God did not give anyone creative faculties for them not to be used. Therefore, it stands to reason that God would have no interest in doing for you what you can do yourself. The reason people think like this is because one of our biggest and often most neglected gifts is our higher, creative faculties. Remember that the human mind is MORE FERTILE than the best soil on earth, and as you sow, you WILL reap. Think of the soil of the earth as an illustration given to us by God of what the human mind is capable of. Plant what you WANT to happen there. Be a good, sincere caretaker of the fertile environment that is your subconscious mind.

This means that if you want things to change, you must DECIDE NOW what you want your life or current circumstances to look like. Leave all the "excuses" or "reasons" that you "can't" out of the equation. You have to see and feel the end result at a deep emotional level. Fall in love with the idea! Make it your sole desire. We are here in our physical bodies to give thought and feeling to what we want to happen. When we align our thoughts and feelings with a deep understanding of our desires, this faith becomes a powerful ally for us to have. So, use faith through understanding to bring about real, positive, tangible change in your life. Once you are on your way and understand this, you can help those around you to understand the proper way to act on faith by your own example. Simply saying it isn't enough. You have to want it, feel it, and see the end result of what you want deep down inside. You have to impress it on your subconscious mind by playing out the scene of what you want over and over. Be the star, and enjoy the play! Properly used, the faith inside you combined with a deep understanding is more powerful than anything on earth. Use this faith to create your own reality around what you desire. Another way of looking at it is as Stella Adler said: "If you experience nothing, you have made a dead choice. It doesn't warm you. It doesn't agitate you. You have to choose something that will awaken you." Find that which awakens and excites you, and begin living it NOW.

Things You Can Do That Will Change Your Life Now

One of the actions that brings the most of what you don't want into your life is negative thinking. The challenge to getting rid of these patterns is going to be changing some very long-term, sometimes lifelong, habits. One effective way to do this is to pay attention to the words derived from not. Can't, won't, wouldn't, couldn't are examples. In addition, any words or thoughts which cause negative emotions require your attention. As these words are spoken or thought of by you, think of a positive outcome which will replace what you just said or thought about. Make sure that the thought arouses a good feeling inside, and then hang on to it. As you have already read, as the positive thoughts fill your mind, the space for anything negative will diminish. Another way to remove negative thoughts is to remove your attention from circumstances and events that make you feel bad but do not require your attention. In other words, mind your own business. Don't let your emotions be guided by things that do not affect you directly. If it does not concern you, or you are not in a position to make the situation better, offer your thoughts and faith for the best outcome, and let those involved work to make the situation better.

Remember, everything you say about your life either has already become or is being created by what you are saying and feeling right now. Based on everything you have been saying, is your life a journey to prosperity or staying "as is"?

Be honest with yourself and the others around you. It is especially important to be honest with yourself. One of the biggest causes of guilt is being dishonest with yourself. You become the person who manipulates you. You think about many different ways out of a circumstance that you don't want, attempt to convince yourself you can do it, and act on that thought. Meanwhile, that little voice inside, the intuitive nudge, tells you "no way. It won't work." You are not on the right track if your feelings aren't good about what it is you are trying to do. If there is a challenge in your life that you are fearful of, do as you read earlier, and follow the fear. Place an end result in your mind that envisions this challenge as solved and fulfilled. Believe you can have that result, see your life as it is with that result, and act from those feelings. This is where faith in yourself is so important. It allows you to work with the Law of Attraction to make life better in all circumstances. You cannot allow distractions or doubt to cloud the vision of what you understand can be. Lying to yourself will never get you what your heart really wants. It will almost always get you exactly what you don't want. You may see dishonest people with a lot of money. Those people live from the competitive mindset and always see their wealth as having to come from someone else. You will also notice that people who are living in abundance in all areas of their lives are always honest with themselves and others. The truth shall set you free.

You are here in your incredible body to be your own unique person in this experience we call life, and you must allow others to do the same. You were born to be as free as the Spirit in your body. Your happiness must come from within. Remember not to try and control other people or change their vision of the world. Share yours with them, and listen openly to theirs. There is abundance everywhere you look. There is more than enough good to go around. The vision, gifts, and capability inside every person is boundless. So, follow your dream. If it isn't evident right now, find it. Do whatever it takes. If you follow your own desire, you free yourself from needing to try and change the people and the world around you. You will find your purpose this way. You will know you have succeeded by how strongly this purpose pulls you. One of the best quotes I have found on this is, "The strength that holds you to your purpose is not your own strength but the strength of the purpose itself" by Albert E.N. Gray. Align with this purpose, and you will live in harmony with the Universe as others do. This is the only true path to fulfillment and being free. Find your purpose, follow your desire, and delight in the life you have created. Others will then be inspired by you and be in awe of the life you have created. You can help people the most by demonstrating your ability to do this.

You can begin to change now.

By now you are aware that your life is what you have made it to be. It is that way by design. Through the focusing on and shaping of the thought energy that has flowed through you, you have shaped a life that is uniquely your own. If it is not what you want it to be, decide now to change it. Remember that what we talk about is derived from something we think about, and what we think about, we are drawing toward us. The more emotion there is wrapped around that thought, the faster it is "barreling toward you." Be very clear in the conversations you are having and joining. Make sure any conversation you are joining is one that inspires you, not one about the drama around this or that situation. Use the "that's interesting" process to get conversations moving in an inspired direction for you. If the conversation is inspiring you, it is likely inspiring others. Just imagine how powerful that is: several inspired people on the same subject creating an outcome merely by having a conversation they feel good about.

Make a firm, deep commitment to do all that you want to do in life. Life is extraordinary. Enjoy it. You can start from where you are right now. Think of yourself as the main actor in your own play. YOU are in the starring role. It's YOUR life! As Stella Adler said, "The more complete the reality you build for yourself, the more thoroughly you understand the CIRCUMSTANCES of the character and the play, the easier you make it for yourself." Think of the life you want as the perfect play, and build the best reality you can in your mind. Repeat that play on the theater screen of your mind over and over until your subconscious mind accepts this as your desire for this new default way of living. At that point, it will start becoming just for you because it is the center of your deepest desire.

Give much thought to your life and how it is starting to change at this moment. You know you are Mastering Your OWN Life when the voice inside is much louder and clearer than all of the noise and voices outside.

The best measure of success is the joy in your heart. So, if you are feeling joy right now, you are successful right now! Stay locked like a laser on the thoughts and ideas that have you feeling this kind of joy. Let these thoughts be the birth of new ideas that awaken you even further. And enjoy the journey of watching these ideas being born into your reality.

Remember to remain in a creative mindset, and avoid the competitive mindset. The creative people of this planet find their way to prosperity much faster and easier that those who are competitive and think there HAS to be a winner or loser in every aspect of their lives. Remember that wealth that comes from the competitive mindset assumes someone had to lose it for the other to gain it. Here today, gone tomorrow. You really aren't at all interested in the kind of wealth people compete for. Obtain wealth from the one infinite supply for all the Universe, and it is yours to keep and share with others. You move away from the competitors by being a creator. Self-esteem comes from the creative mindset, and the ego comes from the competitive mindset. The most creative people around really don't even have to acknowledge competition; they let their results speak for themselves.

Do you deserve the good life? Of course you do. Look around you, and be excited by the endless opportunities there are to express yourself, and get the most out of the new person you are in this moment. There is literally an infinite supply of life experience for you to appreciate. What a great way to begin this process. The choices are everywhere around you. Go look. See what stands out. Find the experiences that are in tune with your heart. This may lead you to another job, career, or hobby. Whatever it is, it is another vehicle to inner joy. Your inner joy will, by the Law of Attraction, bring more good things into your life. This attracts more joy. This is a great cycle to be in. Once you get the hang of this, people around you will be astonished at the life you live. Go ahead and show them how you did it. One by one, people will start to believe and unlock their true potential. As more people become Unique Renegades, the world will be a better place to live. People inspiring people to prosper. Think about what a wonderful world that will be to live in.

THINKING INTO RESULTS COACHING

In association with the Proctor Gallagher Institute, the coaching I offer as a Thinking Into Results consultant gives a person a set of no-nonsense, powerful skills to get the momentum of your belief system to serve you. Chances are that you have let many people talk you into believing things that you know aren't in harmony with you deep, down inside. What you and everyone on this planet want is the freedom to follow your desires with the best feeling possible. Life is a journey that always presents new opportunities based on the beliefs you have. Are your beliefs serving you? If not, let's get the momentum going YOUR way!

Please see **http://miketate.com/services/thinking-into-results-coaching/** for more details.

ABOUT THE AUTHOR

Mike Tate, Master of Inspired Thought

So, who is this "Master of Inspired Thought"? My name is Mike Tate. I live a life that allows me to easily summon the answers to questions from pure, Inspired Thought. These answers are Divine and allow me to see things in my reality for what they actually are. I have used this clarity to create an excellent life for myself and those around me. Life is great and always getting better for me.

I have worked with others to help them lead the inspired lives they want to live by showing them the results of using the processes included in this book. Helping others find their own prosperity has always been inspiring for me. I have begun speaking in public about these principles and want to share them with as many people as I possibly can. Being an inspiring example is something that is very important to me.

My biggest desire is to create a reality where the people around me are getting what they want and live the lives they truly want to only because they want to. Because there aren't as many of those people in my reality as I would want (a few million inspired by this book would be good), my desire is to inspire as many as possible to live as they deserve to.